Fiona Fullerton loves property. Known to millions as a film
actress and television presenter, Fiona is also a writer and
property investment guru. For several years she wrote a popular
weekly property column in the *Saturday Telegraph* which
inspired tens of thousands to follow her advice. She now writes
on property for the *Mail on Sunday* and various other
publications. Fiona runs her own successful property business,
buying, renovating and letting flats in London and Oxford.

Recognised for her part in the Bond movie *A View to a Kill*,
Fiona has enjoyed a high-profile media presence for over 20
years. She lives in Gloucestershire with her husband Neil
Shackell, two children, two dogs and two cats.

Also by Fiona Fullerton

How to Make Money From Your Property

FIONA FULLERTON'S

GUIDE TO

BUYING, SELLING & MOVING HOUSE

FIONA FULLERTON'S

GUIDE TO
BUYING, SELLING & MOVING HOUSE

PIATKUS

Copyright © 2003 by Fiona Fullerton

First published in 2003 by
Judy Piatkus (Publishers) Limited
5 Windmill Street
London W1T 2JA
e-mail: info@piatkus.co.uk

The moral right of the author has been asserted

A catalogue record for this book is available from the British Library

ISBN 0 7499 2400 4

Text design by Paul Saunders
Edited by Carol Franklin

This book has been printed on paper manufactured with respect for the environment using wood from managed sustainable resources

Printed and bound in Great Britain by Mackays Ltd, Chatham, Kent

For Neil

Contents

Acknowledgements

I would like to thank the following for their patience, help, research and good humour.

Julian Gore at Edwin Coe, my brilliant solicitor, who gives me so much legal advice and helps me to simplify things.

Betina Coulter for typing everything at lightning speed, her research and boundless energy!

Alice Davis, my editor at Piatkus, for being so encouraging and patient.

Ann Clayton at Lloyds for all her financial advice.

And, of course, all the estate agents, tenants, builders, decorators, plumbers, carpet layers, plasterers, electricians and removal men who have put up with me over the years and provided me with such a rich fund of stories. To all of you I am eternally grateful and would like to say a very big thank-you.

Introduction

The other night I had a dream that I was in the mothers' race at school (an embarrassing event at the best of times) and I was wearing flippers. Well, I admit I'm hopeless at running, but running in *flippers*? So I ended up running backwards.

It seems to me that finding, securing and buying a home is a bit like running in flippers actually, or treading water. We all spend an inordinate amount of time and energy finding the right property in the right place, only to have the deal scuppered because we get gazumped or, worse, the seller takes the property off the market. I've been there. I sympathise. Then there's the chain. You can't move in until they've found somewhere to buy, and so on and so on. No wonder we get stressed.

After 25 years of dealing with property matters as a home-owner, an investor and a landlord, I've probably come across most of the problems that one encounters on the bumpy path to homeownership. If I haven't experienced them personally, then I have been told about them from the readers of my various columns on property in the national newspapers.

And what problems they are too! Good grief. It's enough to make you want to set up home in a mud hut in the Masai Mara. Even though I jest, I think there is a huge part of me that wants a simpler way of life. Don't you?

House prices are ridiculous and we saddle ourselves with enormous loans, too many possessions, too many jobs, rushing around at high speed making rash decisions, all the time being force-fed by the media.

Your home is your sanctuary away from all that pressure. Even if you work from home, as I do, make sure it is in a part of the house that you can shut off when it is time to relax and unwind. This could be simply shutting the door. But your sanctuary, your oasis, should be as important to you as drinking water.

Your home is important to you for three main reasons:

1. it is a home for you and your loved ones

2. it says a lot about you

3. it is a massive investment with huge potential rewards.

All of which means it is not a decision to be made lightly.

In my previous book *How To Make Money From Your Property* the emphasis was very much on how to maximise the potential of your investment and increase the profit as you climb the property ladder. In this book, I am concentrating solely on the buying and selling procedure, and the task of moving house. As the procedure for buying and selling in Scotland differs from the rest of the UK, I shall be dealing with that in separate sections in Chapters 4 and 7. I will not be covering the rental market or buying as an investment, as I feel that those are very different areas and ones that should be addressed separately.

Buying the right property for you, that has immediate market saleability, is the key to this book. Hopefully I can help you make those decisions quickly and efficiently. I'm a great list-maker so you'll see plenty of lists with categories that you can tick off as you go along!

Don't despair. A certain amount of optimism and fortitude is required when buying and selling, and as an old friend keeps telling me, 'Everything happens for a reason.' If you lose the house you really, really wanted, there'll be another one round the corner that will probably suit you better in the long run.

The market changes so rapidly, as does the Chancellor of the Exchequer, that rates and legislation fluctuate with the seasons. But I have tried to be as accurate as possible. This book is not meant to be a guide to conveyancing or to be a substitute for the need to take professional advice; it is merely to help you feel that you have more control when walking into the offices of your solicitor/agent/surveyor/lender.

I've made more blunders in the property market than I care to mention, but each one has taught me something, whether it be to do with the location, the type of building or the length of lease. These mistakes have sharpened my approach and made me more businesslike when it comes to selling and buying.

Remember, the professionals are there to help you, so don't be reticent about asking lots of questions. Hopefully, between us all we can guide you through the minefield of the property market in as smooth a way as possible.

Fiona Fullerton, 2003

PS Please retain your sense of humour at all times. Every crisis has its funny side, believe it or not.

PART ONE

Buying

CHAPTER 1

What do I need to buy?

Deciding what you need to buy

Doing your research

Spotting the potential

My old friend Lolly came to stay the other day. When I say old, I don't mean she's old, it's just that I have known her for a very long time. She's one of those girls who comes to visit us in the country wearing cream sling-backs, a pale suit and an air of sophisticated chaos, while I, on the other hand, am wearing Wellington boots and jeans. For years, she has been telling me how clever I was to get on to the property ladder so early on in my career. (It's only clever with the benefit of hindsight. At the time it just seemed the right thing to do.) She has been renting for nearly 26 years now.

So, the other day she was picking my brains about how to get a mortgage. 'Will I have to give up shopping?' she asked. 'I'm so terrified that a mortgage is going to curb my lifestyle and become a huge millstone around my neck. What shall I do, Fi?'

After making various calculations, I explained to her that her rental was costing her far more than a mortgage and that she could buy a fantastic home and decorate it exactly how she would like to. She looked absolutely thrilled. She is now deciding what to buy and where, and can be found haunting various estate agents around London.

Deciding what you need to buy

Deciding what you need to buy as opposed to what you really want are two very different things. For the first-time buyer, the decision to purchase a home of your own is not only an enormous financial undertaking, it should also fill you with joy and anticipation. If you have been renting for the past few years, imagine the thrill of being able to paint the walls that fabulous aubergine colour you have been lusting after ever since you saw it in Habitat. You can hang pictures wherever you want to without the landlord screaming about the holes that you are making in his recently replastered walls.

Your average monthly outgoings will probably be lower than they were when you were renting and you can even get a pet gerbil without fear of breaking the rules. In short, this is your castle and you can do what the hell you like with it. But first of all, you need to make a list of the basic criteria that will fulfil your needs. The city centre may be beyond your pocket at present, so here is a brief guideline to help you make those decisions.

- Do you want to live in the country, in town or in a city?

- Do you want a house or a flat?

- Do you want freehold or leasehold? ('Freehold' means you own the land on which the property stands. 'Leasehold' means you have a lease on the property for a number of years, which is granted by the freeholder of the land. So you own the property but not the land. Most flats are leasehold.)

- Do you want a brand-new home or an old one?

- Do you want privacy and seclusion or do you want to live on an estate within a bustling community?

- Do you want a flat in a serviced block?

- Do you want a purpose-built flat or a conversion?

- Do you want something to restore or something perfect?

- How many people will be living in the house?

- Are you expecting to start (or expand) a family?

- Do you need self-contained, separate accommodation?

- Do you want a garden?

- Do you need off-street parking or a garage?

- Do you need stables (ooh, how grand) or a paddock?

- Would you like extra acres with your property? If so, how many?

- Do you want a sea view or a riverside location?

- How many bedrooms do you need?

- How many reception rooms would you like?

- How many bathrooms would you like?

- Do you need to be close to schools?

- Do you need to be close to a mainline railway station?

- What is your maximum journey time to work?

- Do you need special disabled access?

- Do you want to be able to let out a room to help pay the mortgage?

- Are you buying to rent?

- Do you want to purchase a second home?

This list is designed to help all homebuyers and not just first-time buyers. For example, if you are relocating for work reasons you would be wise to consider all the various options.

Living in town versus living in the country

I am a bit of a country bumpkin myself, as readers of my newspaper columns will have gathered. Having had a rather peripatetic childhood being dragged from one exotic country to another, I can safely say I am happiest when at home in the English countryside. But this is not for everyone. I have townie girlfriends who come to stay for the weekend, with perfectly manicured nails, who marvel at my simple way of life but who would rather stick pins in their eyes than be more than 200 metres from the shops.

Reasons for buying in the country

There are obvious reasons for wanting to live in the country:

- unpolluted air;

- quieter environment;

- country walks;

- the natural beauty of the countryside;

- often more land with your home, so more space for the children to play in;

- great for gardeners;

- insurance rates are lower;

- pace of life is slower;

- community spirit is stronger;

- more contact with your neighbours.

Reasons for *not* buying in the country

Much as I love the countryside there are obviously going to be reasons why it doesn't appeal to everybody. Singletons, for example, might find it exceptionally lonely and could be much happier in an urban environment. Also:

- the weather can be really ghastly in winter;

- villages can get snowed in;   ▶

- farmyard smells can be really unpleasant;

- places of outstanding natural beauty can attract too many tourists;

- large, detached houses can be expensive to heat;

- planning permission can be restrictive;

- there may be no mains drains or gas;

- there may be no public transport;

- you may need a second car for the family;

- shops and facilities may be miles away;

- schools may be limited;

- social life may be lacking;

- entertainment and sports facilities may be limited.

Good investment in the country

These properties will always provide a good return on your investment when you come to sell:

- sea view;

- stone farmhouse;

- on the edge of a village;

- cottage with charm;

- good-sized family house;

- bit of land;

- thatched cottage;

- detached;

- outside a market town;

- a rectory or vicarage.

Bad investment in the country

These are the types of properties to avoid:

- anything too remote;

- under a flight path;

- house near an industrial area;

- a farmhouse too close to the dairy;

- anything with shared access, such as farm tracks;

- an historic house soon to be surrounded by a new development;

- anything with a history of flooding;

- on the edge of a cliff.

Reasons for living in town

An addiction to carbon monoxide is a very good reason for not wanting to live in the country. Some of my friends get palpitations if they stay away from town too long, because:

- there are more flats available;   ▶

- there is better public transport;

- there are more schools;

- there are better leisure facilities;

- shopping is easier;

- terraced properties are cheaper to heat;

- you will be connected to mains drains and mains gas;

- there is a better chance of cable telecommunications;

- there is less unemployment.

Reasons for not living in town

You may decide against living in town because:

- making friends can be difficult;

- prices are higher;

- space is at a premium;

- there may be no garage or garden;

- you may get lots of noise from traffic;

- parking may be difficult;

- insurance rates are higher;

- the pace of life is faster.

Good investment in town

You might not get as much space for your money but for those committed urban dwellers here is what you should buy:

- a flat with a terrace or balcony or garden;

- riverside warehouse conversion;

- a flat with a parking space;

- something close to all amenities;

- long-lease flat;

- a trendy new development;

- close to a park;

- freehold house, if you can find one.

Bad investment in town

As long as the location is good it is fairly difficult to make a bad investment in any town or city. However, there are the obvious exceptions:

- basement flat;

- can't walk to the shops;

- nowhere to park;

- very short lease;

- no view at all;

- next to a pub or kebab house;

▶

- on a main road;

- history of flooding;

- anything above the third floor without a lift;

- a flat where the common parts have been neglected.

Flats versus houses

According to statistics most people progress to a house from a flat, while working their way up the property ladder. It is still fairly unusual for a first-time buyer to purchase a house, but I understand from several property developers that this is becoming more and more popular as people continue to rent prior to settling down. It all comes down to budget, geography, marital status and available income. If you can afford a house, then buy it, because it will almost always be freehold rather than leasehold and it is more likely to achieve its full market potential.

Things to consider when buying a flat:

- Service charges

- Unlikely to have a garage

- More noise

- Less privacy

- Leasehold

- Leaky roof is freeholder's responsibility

- No stairs

- Can't play loud music

- Can't have pets (sometimes)

Things to consider when buying a flat:

- Buildings insurance

- Will probably have a garage

- Less noise

- More privacy

- Usually freehold

- Leaky roof is your responsibility

- Lots of stairs

- Can play loud music (within reason!)

- Can have pets

Living in a house will inevitably mean extra maintenance costs, which are usually covered by the service charge if you are a flat dweller. If you are going to buy a house you need to think about the potential expense of:

- repointing the walls;

- clearing the gutters;

- fixing the aerial;

- mending the roof;

- sweeping the chimneys;

- repainting the exterior;

- maintaining the garden;

- painting the windows;

- installing a damp-proof course.

If you are thinking of buying a house try to work out in advance what your quarterly bills will come to and then take into account all maintenance. This should then be added to your borrowings so that you can budget what your outgoings will be.

What to look for when buying a flat

Dos

- Do buy a flat with a terrace or balcony, or a garden flat.

- Do buy a flat with a nice view.

- Do buy a flat in a modern riverside development.

- Do buy a flat in a mansion block (remember the service charges).

- If you must buy a garden flat make sure it has good security.

- Do buy a flat in the smart part of town.

- Do buy a flat within easy access of all facilities.

Don'ts

- Don't buy a basement flat for reasons of security and lack of light.

- Don't buy a flat on a very short lease.

- Don't buy a studio flat – most people want a separate bedroom.

- Don't buy a flat above the third floor if there is no lift.

- Don't buy a flat next to a pub.

SERVICE CHARGES

When I was living in central London many years ago the service charge on my flat was eye-wateringly huge. Your service charge is usually controlled by the managing agents who take care of the maintenance and running of the block. Sometimes in smaller conversions the service charge is managed by the residents themselves, but in my experience this can lead to complications and disagreements. It is always better to have the maintenance organised by an outside party. Here is what your service charge will cover:

- the cleaning of the common parts;

- the maintenance of any lifts;

- the entry-phone;

- the porters' (if any) salaries;

- pest control;

- buildings insurance;

- the lighting of communal parts;

- general maintenance;

- sinking fund in case of major works.

Freehold versus leasehold

Most houses are **freehold**, meaning a property where you own the land on which the building actually sits. You therefore have no ground rent to pay nor service charges, but may sometimes incur annual charges if you were to own a private road, for example. In Scotland there is no distinction between the two as all property is, in effect, freehold, although this term is not actually used. (For more on Buying and Selling in Scotland see the relevant sections in Chapters 4 and 7.)

A **leasehold** property is where the land is owned by somebody else (the freeholder), but you own the property for the duration of the lease. This most often occurs with flats in large blocks or houses that have been converted into flats. There will also be ground rent to pay and service charges to the management company. (For more on Service Charges see page 19.) If your lease is running out, you have the right to acquire the freehold or a lease for a further 50 years. This right is only available to people who have lived in the property for the previous three years, and is a lengthy and complicated procedure governed by the **Leasehold Reform, Housing and Urban Development Act 1993**. I suggest you take advice from a solicitor who specialises in this field, but for obvious reasons extending your lease or indeed buying a share of the freehold will definitely increase the value of your property.

Before you buy a leasehold property, try to anticipate how long you might be living there because anything under 50 years is getting a bit risky. Mortgage companies do not like short leases either and will be less likely to lend you the money.

Ancient abode versus new nest

I can quite understand the allure of a brand new home, having lived in a leaky seventeenth-century pile for the last few years.

Buying an old house has its obvious charms and history, but there is a lot to be said for twenty-first-century plumbing. Old family houses are much in demand at present as there are simply not enough of them to go around. Developers have even taken to building houses that look as if they have been around for centuries but with all mod cons, which strikes me as a brilliant combination, but as a nation we will always be divided into two clearly defined groups, namely those who like wonky floorboards, a bit of history and some authentic architectural features, and those who prefer double-glazing, smooth walls and decent plumbing.

Having said that, some old houses provide ideal family accommodation. The Victorians certainly knew how to build a house and they make perfect family homes. They are roomy and spacious, are very easy to convert and will suit an interior that can be either truly traditional or cutting edge contemporary. Most Victorian houses are not **listed** either, which gives you a lot more freedom for conversion. (See page 23 for more on Listed Buildings.) Georgian houses, on the other hand, are usually listed and therefore come with many restrictions as to what you can and cannot do. An old house will usually hold its value and be a very good investment as long as it is sympathetically maintained. A new house on a modern development will not achieve the same capital growth despite its obvious attractions.

Should you buy a new nest?

Pros

- efficient central heating;
- all modern facilities;
- state of the art kitchen design; ▶

- low maintenance;

- good value for money;

- fabulous bathrooms;

- good security;

- you can move straight in;

- 10-year builders' warranty.

Cons

- slower capital growth;

- no history;

- less character and architectural charm;

- possible teething troubles;

- garden unmatured;

- less individual;

- may have restrictive covenants;

- the rest of the development may be unfinished.

Even a diehard lover of ancient buildings, such as me, has to admit to the cons as well as the pros of living in a bit of history.

Should you buy an ancient abode?

Pros

- interesting architectural features;

- mature garden;

- has a history (and maybe a ghost like we do);

- will sell well;

- good capital growth;

- is unique.

Cons

- high maintenance costs;

- possible wood infestation;

- high heating bills;

- higher insurance;

- may have restrictive covenants;

- may be listed;

- more things can go wrong.

Listed buildings

A **listed building** is one that is deemed by English Heritage and/or the local council to be of great historic or architectural importance. There are definite advantages and disadvantages to living in a listed building. The main advantage is that your house will be of special interest. The disadvantage is that you can't do anything without listed-building consent, which is different to obtaining planning permission, and even the smallest of home improvements may cost more than you would expect for a non-listed property. This is due to the special materials involved. For example, lime mortar will enable the building to breathe naturally whereas modern plaster will not. But fear not. There is a huge market for 'interesting' houses and assuming any work is carried out sympathetically and correctly, you should always be able to get your money back, and more.

There are about 530,000 listed buildings in the UK (460,000 in England, 25,000 in Wales and 45,000 in Scotland) and most of them were built before 1840. The listings are split into three categories:

Grade I: These buildings are of paramount interest in a national context, and are mostly churches and public buildings.

Grade II* (with a star): These are considered to be of outstanding interest but usually in a more local context.

Grade II (without a *): These are of special interest and should be maintained and preserved. More than 90 per cent of all listed buildings fall into this category.

Don't be nervous about taking on a listed building as the results will be well worth it. However, to avoid getting into a wrangle with the local council, it is wise to ask for advice and permission before you do anything.

A house that falls within a **Conservation Area** will also be subject to special building consents. A conservation order can apply to a whole town, village or even part of a street and no part of a property can be demolished without permission. Even trees

VAT AND GRANTS

Restoration and renovation is VAT exempt on some listed buildings when it is with buildings consent from the local authorities.

There are grants available for restoration but only if the building is considered to be 'at risk'. Grants are usually not available for standard home improvements – even to a listed building – unless there is no internal sanitation. Grants for disabled facilities etc. vary from council to council, so it is best to make applications and seek advice. As soon as you ask for a grant you will have to comply with all English Heritage and Listed Buildings Regulations.

within a conservation area are subject to preservation orders. My advice would be not to do *anything* without first seeking advice from the local authorities, because breaking the rules is a criminal offence. When your solicitor makes his local search it will show whether the property you are interested in is a listed building or in a conservation area.

Here are my tips for dealing with a listed building.

- Remember, there is no such thing as a 'typical' listed building.

- Always seek advice.

- There are various grants available – from English Heritage and the Heritage Lottery Fund – for owners of Grade I and Grade II* properties who wish to restore a building that is derelict or has no indoor sanitation. (See Useful Addresses.)

- The local council can provide you with names of builders who are experienced in conservation work.

- A listed home will not affect your mortgage application.

- Most buildings pre-1840 tend to be listed.

- Always get listed buildings consent.

- Read up on the history of your property.

- A listing applies to both the inside and outside of the property.

- Ask the relevant society for advice (such as the Georgian Group or the Victorian Society). (See Useful Addresses.)

Doing your research

It always amazes me how little research and effort people put into buying a new house. They spend more time researching a fridge/ freezer on the internet than they do the location and environment of their future home. A girlfriend of mine bought a flat in South London several years ago only to discover, to her horror, that she lived beneath a famous musician. Needless to say, he was prone to rehearsing at six in the morning.

Similarly, my parents moved to Cheltenham only to discover that the train service to Central London took for ever and left a great deal to be desired. These are fundamental mistakes when it comes to buying your home. Doing your homework is crucial if you are to avoid making a costly mistake. Whether you are buying a flat or a house, in the town or in the country, here are a few questions for you to follow up before putting in an offer.

- How far is the nearest supermarket?

- Is the house near a railway line or main road?

- How far is the station?

- Can you walk to work?

- Do you have noisy neighbours?

- Can you park after work?

- Is your street well lit?

- Do you feel safe? Try the walk from the tube or bus stop at night to see how secure you feel.

- Are you next to a noisy farm (you may want to shoot that cockerel)?

- Where are the schools?

- How long does the school run take?

- Are aeroplanes skimming your chimneys?

- Are you close to a river that is prone to flooding?

- Does the area have a high crime rate?

- Which council tax band are you in?

- Check the regular journey times if you commute.

- Where is the nearest pub?

- Do the roads get congested in summer?

- How close are all local amenities?

- Do the neighbours remind you of the Munsters?

Remember that when buying in the country most of these elements are crucial. If you have teenage children be prepared for the fact that you will become a regular taxi service as they get older. Also, restaurants may be few and far between, and shopaholics may find they are getting withdrawal symptoms from the plentiful choice of the city. Another friend of mine moved from London to Kent and back to London within the space of 18 months, costing her husband a small fortune in stamp duty and legal fees, simply because she couldn't find a decent frock shop.

> **ANY ONGOING PROBLEMS?**
> It may be worth asking your solicitor to make sure that there are currently no legal disputes with your soon-to-be neighbours, regarding party walls, trees, access rights etc. You don't want to inherit an ongoing problem.

Spotting the potential

Use your imagination. So what if the property looks a little run down? In my experience, the secret to making money out of property is to buy what nobody else wants and then turn it around into something that *everybody* wants. Believe me, this isn't as difficult as it sounds. The trick is all about spotting the potential of the property.

Try to view each home as a potential blank canvas. Obviously this is easier in an empty property, recently painted, devoid of any personality. But when you walk into a flat or house that makes you want to laugh immediately because of its hideous bad taste, please don't overlook its potential. That ghastly carpet could actually be distracting you from the beautiful architectural features within the room. Look beyond the collection of porcelain rabbits and imagine what the property would look like once it has been emptied. All too often, we as buyers are more influenced by other people's lifestyles than we are by the potential space, light and structural possibilities of the property. The obvious things to look for are basic dimensions of the room, ceiling height, windows – does it have attractive bay windows, for instance – staircase, floor tiles, wood floors, fireplaces, cornicing and views.

I have been known to lift a corner of the carpet in the sitting room to take a sneaky peak at what lies below. You'd be amazed how many Victorian houses have exquisite tiled floors lurking beneath some mouldy old Formica. And with wood flooring being all the rage at present, it may be worth stripping the carpets out altogether and hiring a sander for the weekend.

Windows are also an important feature that can so easily be hidden by ghastly curtains. Make sure you take a good look at the full window height and width. Fireplaces are a wonderful focal point in a room and you may stumble across a property where they have been boarded up or blocked in.

'STICKERS'

Ask an estate agent to show you a house that has been 'sticking' on the market for a while and then ask them why it's not selling. It could simply be that no one has spotted its potential.

Even the most derelict of houses have the potential to make wonderful homes but these are certainly not for the faint-hearted because of the months of sheer hard work and builders' hassle that you will have to endure. The problem is, most of us want to be presented with a home that is ready to move into, but in a rising market or with a limited budget you would be wise to use a little imagination in order to see the possibilities and make a healthy profit.

What to look out for

- Look for interesting features, such as fireplaces, wood floors and windows.

- Ignore the décor and the furniture.

- Use your imagination.

- Ask the agent how much they think it might be worth after you have done it up. ▶

- Assess the space and light.
- Don't be afraid to be nosy; lift those carpets, push those curtains aside.
- Tangerine walls and avocado bathrooms should not deter you. They can easily be rectified.
- Remember the location.
- Is the loft space suitable for conversion?
- Does it have a big enough garden to do an extension?

CASE STUDY

Brian Freeman told me about his love affair with pebble-dash! He has purchased several houses over the years that had the sort of exterior that immediately put people off. (See Kerb Appeal on page 160.) He sought out boring 1950s architecture smothered in unattractive pebble-dash. As a self-employed builder he could see how simple it would be to transform the exterior to appeal to a wider market.

He only bought houses that had good light and then set about rendering the walls to a lovely smooth finish, painting them cream and the front doors navy blue. He gave the interiors a whitewash, presenting clean, attractive homes to his buyers. He never failed to sell quickly and at a very healthy profit. This is a good example of someone using his imagination to spot potential.

Identifying an up and coming area

I always call this 'Spotting the new coffee bars'. Why? Because if a new coffee bar has suddenly appeared in an otherwise undesirable area, it usually means that the developers are moving in. A little bit of sleuthing goes a long away to identifying an area that will soon be hot in the market. For example, improved transport links are guaranteed to spread residential areas into otherwise undeveloped locations; areas adjacent to already popular boroughs are worth looking at; new tourist attractions will inevitably put house prices up.

When the Eden Project near St Austell in Cornwall was first discussed, long before development, the smart investor would have purchased a property close by knowing that its value would increase once the Eden Project had opened. I have friends who bought a little cottage down there simply as a rental investment because of the influx of tourists they were expecting.

Similarly, Paddington in West London has been undergoing a massive regeneration scheme and development in the last few years. When I used to live in West London I never considered Paddington as a good place to buy. Now I wish I had.

Many years ago, Liverpool Docks would have been the last place that some people would want to live. Now lots of people want to live there!

See what I mean? It's all about getting in there quickly, before the major development has begun.

CHECKLIST

Are the transport links being improved? ☐

Have you heard about a new tourist attraction? ☐

Is it adjacent to an already popular area? ☐

Are there disused warehouses in the area? ☐

Is it becoming trendy? ☐

Are the artisans moving in? ☐

Is a by-pass being planned? ☐

Have you done your sleuthing? ☐

CHAPTER 2

What can I afford?

Doing the sums – how much can I spend?

Other costs and hidden costs

The different ways of borrowing money

Applying for a mortgage

This is a crucial question as overstretching yourself financially is never amusing and can lead to very stressful times. No matter what your budget may be, the estate agent is guaranteed to show you a property that is a little bit more expensive, which you are bound to fall in love with. This has happened to us all. It can be most disheartening, so I would recommend that you only go to see properties that fall within your budget.

Doing the sums – how much can I spend?

If you are currently renting, it is more than likely that your mortgage will be less than your rent per calendar month. However, some building societies are happy to lend you up to four times your annual income, but be aware that this can lead to a situation where you have nothing left for those unforeseen circumstances, such as your car blowing up on the M25. Therefore the general rule is that your mortgage repayments should not exceed one-third of your monthly net income, after tax.

If you are single, simply multiply your gross income by three. However, if you and a partner are entering into a joint mortgage, there are two possible ways of estimating the amount you can borrow:

3 × major income + 1 x minor income

or

2.5 × joint income

This is fairly straightforward, but you must take into account all of your monthly expenses. A girlfriend of mine bought her pad recently but failed to take into account that she likes a glass of wine or two and spends approximately six hours every day on her mobile phone. Consequently, she is now pleading poverty to her bank manager! Here is a list that should help you take everything into account (actually, I always have a little bit put aside for contingencies):

Monthly income £

Net monthly salary (first applicant)

Net monthly salary (second applicant)

Overtime, bonuses etc.

Other income

Total income

Monthly expenses

Food and drink		Standing orders/direct debits	
Clothing		Other loan repayments	
Household items		Regular savings	
Entertainment		Life insurance	
Telephone		Household maintenance	
Car and travel expenses		Home insurance	
TV licence/satellite cable sub		Electricity	
Mobile phone		Gas	
Subscriptions		Other fuel	
Holiday fund		Water rates	
Credit cards		Council tax	

Total expenses

Available income each month   **TOTAL**

Total monthly income less total monthly expenses

For example,   your monthly income is   £1,200

your monthly expenses are   £ 700

the difference is   £ 500

The deposit

The deposit is your initial down payment of savings, which will help to keep the mortgage lower. This should be as much as you can afford or have saved, as most building societies will not want to lend you more than 85 per cent of the property's value anyway.

You will be asked for a deposit of up to 10 per cent of the purchase price when you exchange contracts and this can be provided either from your own savings or from the lender.

> Value of property £100,000
> Your deposit £12,000
>
> Therefore your mortgage £88,000

Other costs and hidden costs

Quite apart from your loan there are several major costs involved when buying a property that must be taken into account well in advance. For example, one of the most expensive fees will be your **solicitor**'s. Some charge a fixed fee for conveyancing but it is worth shopping around to find the best quote. Allow for up to 1 per cent of the purchase price plus VAT (see Chapter 4 for more on Solicitors).

Searches and disbursements are extra costs charged by your solicitor and these will include your Land Registry fee to register the property in your name.

Land Registry fees

Price of house	Land Registry fee
£0–£40,000	£40
£40,001–£70,000	£70
£70,001–£100,000	£100
£100,001–£200,000	£200
£200,001–£500,000	£300
£500,001–£1,000,000	£500
£1,000,001–£5,000,000	£800
Land Registry fees in Northern Ireland	
Up to £10,000	£100
£10,001–£20,000	£150
£20,001–£40,000	£200
£40,001–£200,000	£300
£200,001–£300,000	£400
Over £300,001	£500

Land Registry fees in Scotland

These are also based on house cost, but this is divided into much smaller bands. For example, for a house worth £20,000–£25,000, the fee would be £55 and for a house worth £35,000–£40,000, the fee would be £88.

Other costs

- **Stamp duty** is a tax that you have to pay to the government when you buy a house. Any property costing less than £60,000 is exempt and some more expensive properties in targeted inner city areas are also exempt. The payments are:

£60,001–£250,000	= 1% on the whole of the purchase price
£250,001–£500,000	= 3% on the whole of the purchase price
£500,001+	= 4% on the whole of the purchase price

Therefore, on a £70,000 house the stamp duty will be £700.
On a £260,00 house the stamp duty will be £7,800.
On a £600,000 house the stamp duty will be £24,000.
(For the equivalent rates of stamp duty in Scotland, see page 125.)

- A **structural survey** is required by your lender and is usually a safeguard anyway for your own peace of mind. Costs can range from £250 to £1,000, depending on the type of survey you choose. (For more on Surveys see Chapter 4.)

- A **valuation fee** is based on the price of the house plus VAT and will vary according to the lenders' arrangements with the valuers.

- A **mortgage arrangement fee** is payable on nearly all fixed rate mortgages.

- **Life assurance cover.** The lender will need some sort of insurance in case of death of the borrower.

- **Buildings and contents insurance.** A lender will insist that the building is insured against fire etc., but whether you insure the contents is up to you.

- **Estate agents' commission.** (See Chapter 3 on Choosing an Estate Agent.) Commission varies from 1.75 to 3 per cent plus VAT up and down the UK, and only the seller pays this.

- **Removals**. (See Chapter 9.) This cost depends on the quantity of belongings being moved, the distance the van has to travel, the number of men required and the number of days packing.

- **Maintenance fees**. Does the roof need fixing?

- **Council tax**. The local authority offices will tell you what the current annual charge is for the type of building you are buying.

- **Service charges**. These will apply if you are buying a leasehold flat. (See Chapter 4.)

- **Household bills**. Most estate agents and financial advisers have budget planners that can help you work out your monthly expenditure.

- **Water rates**. Or metered charges for water and sewage disposal.

The different ways of borrowing money

OK. So here comes the boring stuff. It's commonly known as the Mortgage Minefield because there are over 3,000 different mortgages currently available in a hugely competitive market. There are also loans and co-operative schemes and, of course, co-ownership, but we'll start with mortgages.

Where to get a mortgage

There are many different places where you can get a mortgage or a loan, as follows:

- building societies;

- banks;

- centralised lenders;

- direct lenders;

- local authorities – if you are buying a council house;

- finance houses and credit companies;

- your employer (if you work for a financial institution);

- some developers and builders can arrange a loan for you on a new build, allowing you to move in for a down payment of only £99.00, for example;

- Independent Financial Advisers (IFAs);

- mortgage brokers;

- internet comparison sites (see Useful Addresses).

Building societies, banks and lenders

As I have said before, doing your research and shopping around will most definitely benefit you in the end, particularly with regard to penalty clauses, which I will come to later. There are so many lenders in the UK now that I suggest you let your fingers do the walking. Internet access means that you can do a lot of your research at home!

Some of the most cost-effective mortgage providers are the UK's least well-known **building societies**. They don't spend millions on advertising budgets and high profile high street outlets and therefore can offer you a 'no-frills', straightforward deal. The magazine *What Mortgage?* is a mine of information concerning the UK's best and worst mortgage lenders and will advise you on current deals being offered by various building societies up and down the country. Don't be swayed by the famous names.

All the high street **banks** offer mortgages and are able to offer a wider range of products because of their size. Some building societies cannot offer you anything more than a small fixed range and might not be able to offer special discounts. Banks can usually offer you all of this and more. The major high street names get most of their funding on the world's money markets and the smaller lenders will find it hard to compete. Therefore, banks are the main source of long-term fixed rate mortgages.

There are many other lenders such as **centralised lenders** who specialise in mortgages for quite specific markets, such as people who are self-employed, but as with all other deals check the redemption penalties and see how their rates compare to other lenders. They can offer very competitive deals, simply because they work from one central location and do not have expensive high street offices.

The trend today is leaning more and more towards **direct lenders** because of the internet and the advent of telephone banking. This makes life relatively easy as you can arrange your entire mortgage without moving from your armchair. These are called '**direct mortgages**', and there is no middleman between you and your mortgage application. You simply complete the application over the phone and your application can be vetted and approved while you wait. The form is then sent to you to sign and the rest of the buying procedure continues as normal.

Local authorities can provide mortgages to council tenants who want to exercise their 'right to buy' option.

Finance houses may be prepared to secure a loan on a property, but this will usually be at a higher rate of interest and their redemption penalties may be higher, as with **credit companies**.

Your **employer**, particularly if you work for any financial institution, may offer you a mortgage, usually at low interest rates as a fringe benefit. However, be sure to check what would happen if you were to leave your job.

Developers and builders sometimes offer to arrange mortgages for prospective buyers with tempting offers such as '£99 and move in' or part exchange with your existing home. They might offer you 100 per cent mortgages with lower than normal interest rates for the first year, as an inducement to buy. Proceed with caution and take advice.

Independent financial advisers (IFAs)

Beware the dodgy IFA. Receiving completely impartial financial advice can be difficult because everybody is trying to sell you something. Even an independent adviser will want to sell you life assurance, endowment mortgages and pensions for which they receive hefty commissions. IFAs are bound by law to give you the best advice relating to your mortgage but not for selling the mortgage itself. IFAs are regulated by the Personal Investment Authority and by the Financial Services Authority, but it is always best to find one through a personal recommendation. Because they receive commission on various financial products, it is possible that this may influence the way they guide you towards your particular needs.

Mortgage brokers

A mortgage broker will help to find you the best available mortgage that suits your particular circumstances. With 3,000 mortgages available, their knowledge should help to narrow the field. If you don't like what you are hearing you should go to another mortgage broker for a second opinion (a bit like going to the doctor). Mortgage brokers are not allowed to sell you any investment products unless they are an IFA as well.

Going direct

If you already have a good relationship with your building society, then why not stick with them? It simplifies things and they will take you through the various options. Each society has its own guidelines and conditions but some managers are in a position to negotiate on these, so it always pays to ask around before making any commitments.

> Always get independent advice before you sign on the dotted line.

Applying for a mortgage

There are basically only three things that could affect whether you will get a mortgage or not:

1. **Income.** Whether employed or self-employed, do you earn enough to pay for your chosen property? How many other outstanding loans and finance deals do you have? How much do these loans impact on your monthly outgoings? Can you afford to pay all the fees involved in house buying?

2. **Credit history**. Do you have a bad credit rating because you have defaulted on any payments? Have you ever been bankrupt? Do you have a County Court Judgment (CCJ) against you?

3. **The property itself**. Is it in such a state of disrepair that it is structurally unsound and will cost a lot of money to rectify?

When you are applying for a mortgage there are several documents you will need to take to your mortgage lender, so that they can look into your financial and employment history, to ensure that all the details you have supplied are correct.

The more ID and documents you have with you the better, especially if you're in a hurry to raise that loan.

To identify who you actually are, always take your National Insurance number to the potential lender, as well as any of the following documents:

full UK/EC driving licence ☐

valid passport ☐

cheque guarantee card (with photo ID) ☐

marriage certificate ☐

armed forces ID card ☐

signed known employer's ID card ☐

You will also need to provide details of where you have lived for the last three years, so you will need to take at least one of the following:

council tax bill ☐

gas, electricity or phone bill ☐

medical card ☐

bank or credit card statement ☐

current mortgage statement (if applicable) ☐

Inland Revenue tax code statement (for this year) ☐

Bank or other statements must not be more than three months old and should be originals, not copies. You will usually be asked to supply contact details of your employer so the lender can obtain a reference. You will also need to provide proof of your income and your ability to pay the mortgage. For this you will be asked for the following:

WHAT TO DO IF YOU ARE REFUSED A MORTGAGE

If you are turned down by the lender, it could be for any number of reasons and you are entitled to ask. It may be because of the condition of the property being deemed too risky, or because of your occupation. Your credit history could be a deciding factor but if you have had a bad report you are entitled, for a small fee, to see a copy of your record. If your circumstances have changed, you can ask a different lender to consider your application as they may well have different lending criteria.

last three payslips (for both applicants if applying for a joint mortgage) ☐

last P60 (for both applicants) ☐

current account details (for making direct debit payments) ☐

last three years of accounts (if you are self-employed) ☐

rent book (if you have one) ☐

details of your current or last mortgage (if you have one) ☐

information on any pension plan or life insurance policies ☐

details of your monthly expenditure (such as rent, bills, loans, standing orders and so on) ☐

details of any investment accounts you hold ☐

Once you have all these the lender will be able to give you a **decision in principle** – a tentative agreement saying that should you want to borrow X amount they will lend you the money (due to some circumstances, they are entitled to change their minds). The positive side of having a decision in principle is that it can speed things along once you have found a property that you wish to buy and helps to convince the estate agent that you are a serious buyer.

The costs

There are various costs involved, quite apart from the mortgage itself and these are as follows.

- **The arrangement fee**. This is a fee charged by the lender to cover their time and administration costs involved in setting up your mortgage. Some lenders waive this charge and some will let you add it to your loan.

- **Lender's valuation or a valuation survey**. Before the lender will agree to lend the buyer the funds to purchase the house, they want to satisfy themselves that the house is worth the asking price and that their money is secure in the investment. Some waive this fee too.

- **The deposit**. This is your down payment as explained earlier.

- **The mortgage indemnity guarantee (MIG)**. If you are borrowing more than 75 per cent of the value of the property.

- **Mortgage protection**. This is an additional insurance that protects you against unemployment or an inability to work due to prolonged illness. With this your mortgage will continue to be paid until such time as you are able to work again.

Choosing the right mortgage

Where to begin? Because everybody's circumstances are slightly different, I can only explain to you the various different types of mortgage that are available. There are so many variables here, such as your income, your age, your location, any other loans etc., that make you unique. It may be worth seeking independent financial advice (see page 42).

Repayment mortgage

A repayment mortgage is one that lets the borrower pay the interest plus some of the capital over a set number of years. For the first few years, repayments are mostly paying off the interest, but as the years go by the capital will start to be reduced. As the capital gradually decreases, so does the interest and the payments will gradually chip away at the capital. The repayment period in the UK is usually 25 years and the loan will be repaid within the agreed term. However, you can choose the length of repayment term, but 25 years is usually a lot more manageable than, say, over 15 years.

A repayment mortgage is probably advisable in the following circumstances:

- If you are planning to stay in your new home for quite a while. If you move house frequently your debt will not be very much reduced, because you will be paying mostly interest rather than capital.

- If your granny leaves you a fortune, which you can use to pay off all or part of the loan.

- If you want a mortgage that lasts for less than 10 years.

- If you are not planning to live in the UK permanently for the next 25 years.

Interest only mortgage

The other type of mortgage available is an interest only mortgage. You simply pay off the interest each month but do not touch the capital, which means that by the end of your repayment period you still owe exactly the same amount you borrowed from the lender in the first place. However, as you are not paying off the capital each month, the surplus money that you have is invested in a separate repayment vehicle. There are two kinds of repayment vehicle, an individual savings account (ISA) and an endowment policy. Both of these work in a similar way, in that the money you pay in each month is invested into, and trades on, the stock market. The ISA or endowment provider will advise you as to which sector of the market to invest in and can estimate the return you will get from your ISA or endowment policy. They should be able to calculate whether your savings plan will earn you enough money to pay off the mortgage and how long it will take. In some cases this type of investment can result in your mortgage being paid off early.

Repayment versus interest only

Mortgage:	Type of mortgage	Interest only/ endowment		Repayment	
Loan amount	How much do you want to borrow?	£50,000	£50,000	£50,000	£50,000
Loan term	Length of time for repayment	25 yrs	15 yrs	25 yrs	15 yrs
Interest	The current rate for the mortgage you are interested in	7%	7%	7%	7%
Your monthly payments	How much you will pay per month	£291.67	£291.67	£353.39	£449.41

The endowment policy

'Low cost' endowment policies have received a bad press because they haven't been performing as well as they were expected to and left some borrowers with a deficit in their mortgages. These policies are where the sum insured is less than the amount borrowed but the projected bonuses are supposed to make up the difference. During the economic boom of the 1980s, financial advisers were projecting that long-term interest rates would remain high and that consequently growth would continue to increase, so the return on your investments would adequately cover the cost of your mortgage. Unfortunately, they got it wrong and their vision did not materialise.

An endowment mortgage is investment-linked. You make two separate payments each month with the larger amount being paid to your lender as an interest-only payment. The smaller payment is made to an investment fund run by a life assurance company. The idea is that the money invested will build up over the years allowing you to repay the capital borrowed in one lump sum when the policy matures. Endowment policies have been known to be a fairly risky option depending on the movements of the stock market. A financial adviser will be able to guide you on the current economic strengths and weaknesses of an endowment mortgage.

An endowment mortgage will probably work for you if:

- you are planning to move home fairly frequently as the endowment policy can be moved on to your next mortgage;

- you need a loan for your second home, when you can always take out an additional policy;

- you are prepared to take a small risk because there is no way of guaranteeing that your endowment policy will provide the required sum when it matures.

It can be possible to switch between a repayment and an endowment mortgage if you change your mind or if your endowment policy is not performing very well. However, it is still advisable to shop around before making any final commitments.

You would be wise to only deal with lenders who subscribe to The Mortgage Code – a voluntary code of practice run by the Council of Mortgage Lenders (see Useful Addresses). The code sets out standards of good practice, providing valuable safe-guards for customers.

Flexible mortgage

A flexible mortgage is rather like a bank loan where you can pay off as much or as little as you can afford without being penalised. In other words, if you are feeling flush or have just had a cash windfall you could pay off a lump sum, or if things are a bit tight you could take a 'payment holiday' where you don't pay anything for a while. Flexible mortgages are very popular – particularly with self-employed people as their income can fluctuate – and the rate is usually just above the Bank of England's Base Rate. The interest is calculated on a daily basis.

With some flexible mortgages you can even amalgamate all of your financial commitments, so your savings and your current account are all in the same fund with your mortgage. By doing this, the interest calculated on your mortgage can be reduced, saving you a small sum.

Flexible mortgages have a number of different features:

- a flexible payment scheme allowing you to pay fortnightly or in 10 monthly payments rather than 12;

- the ability to make withdrawals on previous overpayment, or even 'payment holidays' (where you pay nothing for a few months);

- discounted rates or other incentives that can be taken when you want;

- no redemption penalties if you pay off your mortgage.

Paying back the interest

There are five ways of calculating how the interest on your mortgage payments should be made up.

- **Variable-rate mortgage**. Your monthly mortgage payments go up and down with interest rates fixed by your lender. If interest rates fall, your payments go down; if rates rise, they go up. However, this makes it much harder for the borrower to budget the amount that will be coming out of their account each month. This option is usually the least popular but lenders will often try to tempt you by offering attractive cashback deals. But be careful, because this usually means they will lock you into a longer minimum period with hefty penalties if you decide to cash in early.

- **Fixed-rate mortgage**. Your monthly payments stay the same for a specified period, normally one to five years. You can win or lose, depending on the movement of interest rates. If they fall, you are locked in to paying too much; if they rise, you save money. These are very popular with first-time buyers, because the fixed monthly payments mean that they can budget more easily. At the end of the fixed-rate period, most lenders move to a variable rate. (I usually go for a fixed-rate mortgage but got my fingers burnt when interest rates dropped dramatically!)

- **Capped-rate mortgage**. Your monthly payments will never exceed a certain amount. If interest rates fall, payments go down; if rates rise, they are 'capped' at a maximum level. Although theoretically better than a variable-rate or a fixed-rate mortgage, it is rare for the cap to be set at any level biased towards the borrower. Sorry, but these guys have it all sewn up.

- **Discount-rate mortgage**. The discount-rate works by giving the borrower a percentage reduction on their variable rate for a limited period of time. This is usually 2 per cent below Base Rate. The discounted rate changes, as with variable rates, and will not protect your from rate rises, but you will benefit from any falls. The shorter the period, the bigger the discount. This mortgage provides an incentive for long-term investors.

- **Tracker mortgage**. The rate of interest you pay is the Base Rate plus a fixed percentage agreed by your lender. So, if the Base Rate is 5 per cent and your lender's percentage is 0.95 per cent, you pay 5.95 per cent. In this way, the rate you pay 'tracks' the Bank of England rate more closely than a variable-rate mortgage, making it much easier for you to work out your budget.

Penalty clauses

The lender will usually operate all the rates listed above (except for the Variable Rate) over a fixed term and once you have settled with one particular offer, you will be tied into this agreement for that stated period. Any breaking of that tie-in period will result in what is known as a **redemption penalty**. So, if you move your mortgage to another lender or you pay off the mortgage before the set period has expired, you will be fined for breaking the agreement.

This is very important. No one can see into the future and your circumstances might change considerably within that period, so it is always wise to see how long the tie-in lasts for and how much you would be charged if you had to terminate the contract early. Shop around, because some lenders will have lower redemption penalties than others and shorter tie-in periods.

Paying the penalty can be eye-wateringly painful and I should know because on two occasions I've sold a rental investment prior to the five-year deal elapsing. Penalties come in lots of different guises. Some are a fixed amount; others may involve repaying all the savings received on a special deal or even paying up to nine months' interest. Ouch.

To avoid this situation it may be best to simply pay the standard variable rate and decline deals, if you intend to repay your loan quickly or if you think you may move house. Direct lenders – such as via the internet – offer very low standard rates with no penalties for repaying all of your loan and some high-street lenders offer deals with no penalties attached.

A flexible mortgage has no redemption penalties, so is worth looking at.

Scottish mortgages

Loans in Scotland are granted in two main stages. The first is deciding the maximum they will lend you and the second is a question of how much they will lend for a specific property, pending the results of the survey. Scottish mortgages differ from elsewhere in the UK in that they have to be secured *before* an offer can be made on a property.

A valuation will have to be carried out as per usual and you will have to pay a fee for the valuation, even if you don't buy the property.

In return for the loan, you give the lender what is known as 'standard security' over the land and buildings that you are buying (legally known as 'heritable property'). The standard security is a legal document, and it will contain the terms you have agreed with your lender. Your mortgage lender keeps the title deeds to your property until you have repaid the loan in full.

Insurance

Mortgage payment protection insurance (MPPI)

This insurance, known as the MPPI, is needed if you are buying a house as a couple or if anyone is financially dependent on you, were you to die. Pretty morbid, I agree, but necessary nonetheless. Some lenders insist on it, but in fact it is a relatively cheap form of life insurance. This is usually linked to a repayment mortgage as endowment mortgages have life insurance included.

There is another form of mortgage protection policy that will pay your mortgage if you are unable to, due to illness or unemployment.

Read the small print of any policy carefully because there can be all sorts of catches. For example, they won't pay if you volunteer for redundancy; they won't pay if you worked part-time; or if you've been with your employer for less than a certain number of years.

These policies are not cheap and are available from your lender. Check how long they will pay out for, because it is usually only for a year. Also, look out for any exclusions in your policy such as medical conditions you have had before you took it out. Other exclusions might include stress, back problems and pregnancy.

A basic MPPI policy should:
- pay out after a maximum of 60 days;
- provide cover for no less that 12 months after the excess period;
- individually assess medical conditions;
- have a more standardised approach to self-employed and contract workers;
- give at least six months' notice of any change to a policy.

Buildings and contents insurance

Your lender will insist that the building has insurance against fire etc., so as soon as you exchange contracts, ask your solicitor to make sure that a policy is in place. The cost will vary depending on the type of building and where it is. Remember, the policy should be for the **reinstatement value** and not for the current market value of the property. In other words, it needs to cover what it would cost to rebuild in the event of complete destruction. Heaven forbid.

Most lenders will offer to arrange cover for you but they get commission for this. You don't have to go with their choice. Phone around for other quotes.

Your buildings insurance should include cover against:

- fire;

- lightning;

- earthquake;

- explosion;

- accidental damage (such as sticking your leg through the loft floor);

- theft or malicious acts;

- riots;

- storm and floods;

- things dropping off an aircraft;

- subsidence;

- falling trees or branches;

- impact by vehicles;

- breakage or collapse of aerials;

- burst water tanks or pipes;

- escape of oil from heating installations.

(Acts of terrorism are now being excluded from some policies, so if you live in a vulnerable area such as the City of London, you may need to take out extra cover.)

> Leasehold properties are usually insured by the landlord/free-holder and this will be covered by your service charge. Make sure you're not doubling up on your insurance.

The **contents** of your home should be insured separately and some insurers will offer you a discount if you take out both contents and buildings insurance with them. If you already have a contents policy then first notify your insurers of the new address and the date you are to move in.

> Insurance is a very personal, subjective thing. A friend of mine refuses to insure her contents even though she is the owner of some staggering jewels. 'What does it matter, darling?' she says. 'If it's my turn, the buggers will have a hell of a job pawning that lot'.Personally, I go for peace of mind.

QUESTIONS TO ASK...YOUR MORTGAGE LENDER/ BANK/BUILDING SOCIETY

Apart from the obvious questions like 'Are you a shark? Are you going to screw me to the wall?' and 'Are you giving me the best

advice or do you have a hidden agenda?', there are several things
you need to ascertain when enquiring about a mortgage.

Q Is there a standard interest rate and what special deals are
available – and will there will be an arrangement fee?

Q What payment would you have to make per
£1,000 borrowed?

Q When and how your payments would have to be made:
in the first month?
in the rest of the financial year?
thereafter?

Q What will happen when the interest rate changes?

Q What percentage of valuation is the normal maximum loan?

Q What insurance must be bought as a condition of the loan
(contents, buildings, mortgage protection, etc.)?

Q Will there will be a redemption charge if you pay off the
mortgage within so many years. If so, how many years?

Q Does the broker offer 'information only' or an advice and
recommendation service on the best mortgage for your individual needs? This should be disclosed under the Mortgage Code.
You have more comeback if you go for the advice service – and
you are not obliged to accept the advice if you do not like it.

The Mortgage Code of Practice lays down the information the
lenders and intermediaries must give you as the customer. When
seeking advice or approaching a broker always ask whether they
comply with this code.

Filling in the forms

Forms fill me with absolute dread, especially if there are questions that I can't answer immediately. I usually regress to childlike behaviour and start crying, hoping that someone will fill it in for me. However, even though your mortgage application form may look as if it has more small print than a telephone directory, don't despair. Take a deep breath and remember that if you can't answer something, ring your solicitor or lender and they will tell you what to do.

TOP TIPS

Here are my three top tips for filling in the form.

- Always read the small print. Boring but essential.

- Use a pencil to fill it in first, so that any mistakes can be easily rectified. When happy, go over it in black felt-tip.

- Don't leave any questions blank as this will hold up the application procedure. If it doesn't apply to you, just put N/A (not applicable).

Here are a few other things that you will need to know to successfully fill in the form:

Q Ask your lender if your loan has a special code or name.

Q How much are you actually borrowing after you have put down the deposit?

Q How long will the mortgage be for?

Q What is the full address of the new property, including the postcode?

Q Who is your surveyor?

Q What is the ground rent and service charge? (If it is leasehold.)

Q What is the building made of? Cotswold stone, red brick or, God forbid, straw?

Q Is it a flat, maisonette, semi-detached, detached etc.?

Q Who is providing your buildings insurance and what is the policy number?

Q Who is providing your MPPI?

Q Have you ever had a county court judgment (CCJ) registered against you? Or been made bankrupt or been refused credit or failed to make previous mortgage payments? If you have, be honest about it because telling porkies will only be revealed when they do their credit checks.

Q Has a previous application from you been turned down and, if so, for what reason?

The costs of getting a mortgage

These are the costs that will have to be paid by you for the pleasure of borrowing money from somebody who will charge you a huge amount of interest for doing so. Charming isn't it? Here they are:

- the lender's valuation fee;

- an arrangement fee;

- the lender's legal fees;

- your solicitor's fee for handling the mortgage.

Then there are extra costs depending on the type of your loan:

- the MIG (mortgage indemnity guarantee) if you are borrowing more than a certain percentage of the value of the property. This is usually a lump sum;

- buildings insurance;

- premiums for a MPPI.

Joint mortgages and co-ownership

Buying with a friend or partner has its obvious advantages as it means you will be able to borrow much more between you. Usually it is two-and-a-half times the joint income but some lenders calculate it by three times the higher income and one time the lower income.

You may need to shop around because some lenders are a bit fussy about friends buying together.

There are two different types of co-ownership (joint tenants and tenants in common) and if there are more than two people purchasing a property they should buy as 'tenants in common'. This means that they would each own distinct and separate shares of the property and if one dies his share does not go to the others but to his estate. It's important that a Deed of Trust or a Contract is drawn up on exchange of contracts because it will help to clarify the payment of household bills, maintenance and the situation generally if one person was to leave. This Deed of Trust would also specify the amount of each individual investment and how the co-owners would be repaid from the proceeds of a sale if each owner invested different proportions as opposed to equal portions.

It is crucial to have this Deed of Trust in place because no one can foresee the problems ensuing from relationships or friendships. Sometimes you can agree that if one moves out they offer their share to the other.

- Before buying with a friend, examine ruthlessly whether this is a good idea. Legalities such as this can sometimes put enormous pressure on a friendship.

- For simplicity, try to buy in equal portions.

- You are not limited to having two people on the mortgage. You can have up to four people on any one property deed.

- To get the largest mortgage take the two largest incomes to the lender.

- Everyone named on the mortgage deed will be liable 'joint and severally', which means that if one of the co-owners can't meet their payments it will be up to the others to make up the balance.

- If there is a non-payment everyone will be affected by a bad credit record, even those who have paid.

- A Deed of Trust should be drawn up by a solicitor. This will specify details such as individual investment, payment of household bills etc.

- Take out insurance to cover you in case one owner can't work due to illness.

CHAPTER 3

Finding your home

Where to find your property

Less conventional purchases

Estate agents

Understanding floor plans, details and photos

Viewing a property and how to do it

Putting in an offer

How to negotiate

No one said buying a home was easy, but finding it first can be even trickier. There are various ways to search for a property and I have tried them all, trawling through magazines, scrolling through internet sites, calling estate agents and even searching the private ads. You could also look out for 'House for Sale' signs and advertisements in the local papers. You could even let it be known to friends, neighbours and colleagues that you are looking for a home in a particular area. You'd be amazed how word of mouth can be so crucial when looking for a property. A friend of mine had been looking for a house for two years when, out of desperation, she burst into tears at her hairdresser's. As luck would have it, the previous client had been bemoaning the fact that she couldn't find a buyer for her house. Hey presto! Two very happy people. So it pays to spread the word.

Where to find your property

The internet

A huge source of information is readily available on the internet. Every estate agent has their own website and there are specialist sites where you can buy and sell direct. Be very specific with your requirements – the price range, the location, number of bedrooms, whether you need a garage or garden, number of bathrooms etc. – and the relevant properties will pop up for you to choose from. Some sites even have a video walk-through so that you can see right around the house.

Avoid too narrow a price range as this will often mean you will miss out on potentially suitable homes. If too many properties are found when you have keyed in all the information, you can always refine your research further. For example, try a specific postcode or number of bathrooms. Another way around the overload problem is to register with a property site. They will email you as soon as a property matching your criteria appears on the market. Don't expect to find your ideal property by visiting just one site – it is worth registering with several. If nothing suitable comes up the first time around, don't despair; remember it's an ever-changing market. (See Property Websites in Useful Addresses.)

Magazines and newspapers

Geography can present huge problems when buying, because if you live in Suffolk and are looking to buy somewhere in Cumbria, then obviously you are not going to be able to drop everything when the local estate agent says he's got 'the perfect house for you'. This is where magazines and newspapers can be a good source of research through their advertising and editorial pages. If you are relocating, get a friend or a work colleague to send you as much local information as they can on available properties. Most local estate agents have their own gazette or free sheet and local newspapers carry lots of advertising.

Glossy magazines such as *Country Life*, or local glossies like *Shropshire Life* or *Cotswold Life*, show plenty of houses for sale from both ends of the market.

The **national newspapers** all have property sections, which are worth scouring every weekend and you will quickly discover whether the area you are considering is within your budget. The newspapers tend to list their ads by county, which makes things a bit easier.

If your company is moving you to a new location they may employ a special **relocation agent** who will help you to find the right property in the right area. If not, a huge number of agencies offer a countrywide relocation service. There will be a fee for this service, but the agent's knowledge of the local market will help to save you time, money and unnecessary travel.

Buying privately

If dealing with estate agents leaves you cold, then you could always try buying privately, bypassing the agent entirely. There are private ads in most newspapers and, of course, on the internet. They will be accompanied by the seller's telephone number, so all you have to do when an advertisement catches your eye is ring them up and make an appointment to view. However, the trouble is, the seller is bound to be slightly misleading, if not downright elaborate with his or her descriptions, so be prepared for disappointments. Always ask loads of questions before making that journey, e.g. How long is the lease? How many flats in the house? Where is it exactly? What are the neighbours like? Why are you moving? And so on.

Dealing directly with the owner can often be a great way to buy, especially if the seller is in a hurry. It is up to you to do the negotiating, so be firm, otherwise the advantages of bypassing an estate agent are loaded in favour of the seller. The *seller* is the one saving on commission.

Many years ago I was looking for a rental investment in central London, when a private ad caught my eye in the *Evening Standard*. I went to see it and could immediately see its potential, even though it was in a terrible state, having been a student squat for four years. It had turquoise carpet and 1970s bathrooms, but the location was perfect and the seller seemed anxious to be rid of it. Being a bit of demon when it comes to doing a deal, I drove a very hard bargain and got it for a fantastic price.

Also, if you know the street(s) you want to live in, you can always post leaflets through the doors to see if anyone is thinking of selling. This way you get the house and they avoid the agent's fees.

So, I'm all in favour of dealing direct with the seller. It's so much simpler. When you need to ask them a crucial question, you don't need to first ask your solicitor, who asks their solicitor, who asks the seller, who tells the solicitor the answer, who tells your solicitor, who tells you. You can just pick up the phone and say, 'Brian, where do you keep the flipping fuse-box?'

TOP TIPS

Here are my five top tips for buying privately.

1. Ask the seller lots of questions on the phone before you bother to view.

2. Make sure the seller tells you about service charges, ground rent etc.

3. Be prepared to negotiate.

4. Get the seller's solicitor's details.

5. Take someone with you for the viewing, for security.

PERSONAL SAFETY

Security is hugely important when viewing a property that has been advertised privately, particularly if you are female. Without wishing to sound too pessimistic there are a lot of funny people out there and as a single female you would be bonkers to walk into a property with a complete stranger. You must be careful. Always take a friend or colleague with you.

Who owns that empty house?

If you have your eye on a boarded-up, derelict property and want to find out who owns it, this is what you should do. Assuming there is no For Sale board outside, you should contact HM Land

Registry Headquarters (see Useful Addresses), and they will tell you which district office handles the enquiries for that area. You can then contact the relevant district and apply for a copy of the register by completing form 109 (don't worry, it is not that complicated) and return it to the office. For a small fee you will then be sent the details of the last-known owner's name and address.

You can then get in touch with them directly and put your proposal to them regarding the property. It may be that it is the subject of a complicated probate situation, now that granny has died and various siblings are arguing over what to do with the house. If you were to make an offer, it may help them make up their minds.

However, the information may be years out of date, which will lead you nowhere, so your only alternative then is a bit of sleuthing. You could visit the neighbours and ask them if they know anything about the house and who owns it or you could ask at the local post office. If all else fails, a detective agency may be able to trace the owner, for a fee.

Less conventional purchases

There are still other ways of buying a property that are considered less conventional and perhaps more risky. However, they can also represent a bargain, if you do your homework thoroughly. They are:

- buying at auction;

- buying a repossessed property;

- building your own home;

- buying off plan;

- doing a direct swap.

Buying at auction

Buying a property at auction can be a fabulous way to secure a bargain, but you must know what you are doing and it is most definitely not for the faint-hearted. Every time I've been to an auction I feel as if my heart is going to pound its way out of my chest! It is a real adrenalin rush, but it helps if you can have a couple of dry runs so that you know what to expect.

Most property auctions are announced or advertised in the local newspapers or at the local auction house. They are arranged through the estate agent's office and once details have been released you are able to view the property and arrange surveys etc.

The main advantage to buying this way is that you avoid protracted negotiations, as once that gavel has gone down, there is no turning back. The property is sold that day to you, assuming you are the highest bidder, and the accepted bid is the completed contract with completion 28 days thereafter. You can also take comfort in the fact that you have paid a price only one bid higher than the under-bidder.

There is a downside, I'm afraid. The buyer must make all his or her own arrangements prior to the auction – mortgage agreement, valuation, survey, solicitor's fees etc. – and these will inevitably involve expense. As there can only be one successful bidder, all the other bidders will have met these expenses in vain. It's a risk you must be prepared to take.

This is how it works. Once you have found the property you want, make sure with your solicitor that the property is free of any legal problems. Often properties with title problems are those that end up being auctioned. Then you should arrange a survey if you are getting a mortgage. A number of houses with structural problems, which make it difficult to get a mortgage, are put up for auction. The lender will probably want a valuation anyway. The most important, and scary, thing is that you must be in a position to sign the contract in the auction room and to pay the 10 per cent deposit of the purchase price then and there. The guide price is usually the seller's reserve price, so it will only go higher!

You must then be in a position to complete the purchase on the date agreed in the contract. This is usually 28 days from the auction date, so make sure your solicitor has all the legal documents in place.

The auction itself will either be held in the local auction rooms, in a hotel or pub (I've been to one in a pub!), at the agent's offices or at the site. It is usually very fast-paced and will all be over in minutes. It is essential that you keep a cool head and stick to your ceiling price. Don't get carried away with the emotion of it all, as you could end up paying far too much for the property. If you can't cope – quit.

CHECKLIST

Auction checklist

Get a loan agreed. ☐

Decide on the property you want. ☐

Get the survey done quickly. ☐

Have a solicitor check the documentation. ☐

Have 10 per cent of the guide price ready; either a personal cheque or banker's draft. The balance will be required in 14 to 28 days. ☐

Know your financial limit and stick to it. ☐

Get there early so you don't miss your lot. ☐

Bring someone to support you. ☐

Buying a repossessed property

The only downside to buying a property that has been repossessed by the lender is that the lender won't have the same knowledge and information to give you as the previous owner. So there's no point asking them about the neighbours or the drains. Consequently, it is important that you get a thorough survey done and that your solicitor is extra vigilant with his investigations. If you are buying it at auction these expenses may well prove costly if you are beaten to the hammer price.

Buying a repossessed home can sometimes be a very sad experience but it can also provide a bargain. Repossessed properties are normally disposed of in the usual way through estate agents or by public auction, but there is also a commercial list of repossessions that you can buy, which is advertised in the property sections of some national newspapers.

There are usually around 40,000 repossessed homes on the market in the UK and the majority of these used to belong to people who simply overstretched themselves financially. This is why doing the sums is so important. The lending companies and banks will do everything to stop having to take control of a property and insist that communication is vital to prevent it happening. However, more often than not, the homeowner ignores all letters and warnings, and that is when the lenders have to take legal action.

When you are viewing a property through an estate agent you won't necessarily be told that it has been repossessed. However, it becomes painfully obvious when you see the anger and frustration that has been taken out on the poor house. A friend of mine bought a house in such a state that every fixture and fitting had been removed in a fit of pique. She said bathroom tiles, fireplaces and even the ceiling rose had been removed and the whole place had been trashed. This sort of damage can cost a great deal to rectify.

This is when you really need to be able to spot the potential of a property and look past the sadness. Properties from every section of the market are represented, from a humble little terraced house to a detached mansion in Mayfair, and the price will obviously reflect the state that it is in. It is a myth that they go for well below market value and that mortgage companies just want to cover their loan, because everything has a value to somebody and it just depends who is viewing or who is bidding on the day.

> Remember, when you buy a property it is essential to change all the locks, as you don't know how many sets of keys are floating around.

Building your own home

If all else fails you could always build your own home and this needn't be as difficult as it sounds.

The most important thing to do first is to secure a plot of land. Some estate agents have lists of available plots and local newspapers will carry advertisements too. But you could also ask surveyors, architects and planning consultants, or even ask around in the local pub or post office.

The local council's planning department will have the Local Plan, which will help you to discover areas that are available for development.

You will need to get planning permission, of course, so detailed plans will have to be drawn up. This is not exactly a breeze as dealing with architects, project managers, builders and contractors needs a certain amount of knowledge.

However, the alternative is to build a house that comes in kit-form, like building out of Lego! A friend of mine bought one of those green-oak, timber-framed barns that arrived in sections and the manufacturers built it for her. It took no time at all. They come in varying sizes and there are several manufacturers now specialising in 'kit-houses' who include construction in their price. (It doesn't have to be a barn.)

The good thing is you can have the internal layout exactly as you want it. (Refer to magazines such as *Build It* and *Building Your Own Home* for useful addresses.)

'Nothing worthwhile is easy' – remember that when you are up to your ankles in mud!

> Most mortgage companies will lend only on an instalment basis, paying out in stages as you progress through the building process. This is because the risks are greater than buying an existing property.

TOP TIPS

Here are my eight top tips for building your own home.

1. Scour the papers and the agents for a plot of land.

2. Contact the local authority for their development guidelines.

3. Get plans drawn up.

4. Apply for planning permission.

5. Get quotes for kit-houses.

6. Get quotes from builders.

7. Negotiate with your lender.

8. Get a caravan to live in temporarily!

Building your own home means saving quite a bit of money as you will be paying more or less cost price for everything. Let the builder buy all materials, as he will get trade prices. When it is completed, its market value will be 20 to 30 per cent *more* than it cost to build. Not a bad investment.

Buying off-plan

When it comes to buying new houses, buying off-plan (i.e. it hasn't been built yet!) is becoming increasingly popular. Committing yourself at this early stage means you get to buy the property at the initial offer price. During the first phase of development, prices are lower and they increase once the developer has completed a few sales. Once the property is complete you can sell on at a profit or move in knowing it has already made you money.

If you are the first owner of a brand-new house – or flat – on a development, you can also choose the best plot and customise your property according to the choices provided by the developer. You may have a choice of kitchen finish, or tiles or door handles etc. You can even choose how many plug sockets you need. These will all be extras, but should still be value for money. They will have a show home for you to look at so that you can envisage the end result. But don't be fooled by the clever styling. If the house you are looking at is quite small, the designers will have employed all the tricks in the book to create the illusion of space. These include:

- lots of mirrors;
- clever lighting to brighten the space;
- under-scale furniture;
- small beds in bedrooms;

- pale colours;

- beautiful accessories;

- some missing doors.

To get a clearer impression, ask to see a house that is completed but undecorated. This will usually be possible.

The only risk of buying off-plan is if the bottom falls out of the property market, and you find yourself committed to purchasing a house that is now worth less than you paid for it. But this can be true for any property. The other downsides are that the completion dates are usually on the optimistic side. You may find your moving date slips back and you encounter some delays. You will need to scrutinise the plans and find out exactly what will be included to avoid any disappointments when you move in. Also, if you do encounter any problems, make sure you write down your complaints as soon as possible so that they can be rectified by the builder. This process is called 'snagging'.

> Most new estates provide value for money, but developers and familiar building companies do vary a lot in their quality and finish. Have a good look around at what is on offer. Most estates have three or four different companies building on them, to varying standards, so ask any owners who have already moved in what they feel about the build quality.

CHECKLIST

Buying off-plan checklist

Study the property specification carefully. ☐

Ask to see the architect's plans and other working drawings. ☐

Check the square footage and what it includes. ☐

Consider the position. ☐

Check out local property values. ☐

Visit other sites by the same developer and question owners of their houses. ☐

Check the development is covered by NHBC Buildmark Warranty or an equivalent scheme. ☐

If you're buying a flat, ask about service charges and how they are assessed. ☐

Check whether a parking space is included in the price. ☐

Make sure your finances are in order. ☐

Remember you will have to pay a reservation fee, which is non-refundable, but often deducted from the deposit at exchange of contracts. ☐

A 10 per cent deposit is payable on exchange, which you will lose if you fail to complete the deal. ☐

Check with a solicitor before signing any contracts and make sure any special deals you have agreed with the developer are included. ☐

Request a clause which will give you your deposit back if your home is not ready by a certain time. ☐

Doing a direct swap

Finally, there is buying and selling property on the direct swap basis, which can work marvellously to your advantage. The small ads on the property pages have hidden treasures that cut out the agents or you could take out an ad in the local paper of the area in which you wish to buy. For example, 'Do you own a barn near Chippenham? Need a flat in Putney? Why not swap?'

CASE STUDY

A girlfriend of mind swapped houses with her mother-in-law recently because she needed a bigger house and her mother-in-law wanted a smaller home. They both lived in the same town and after a brief discussion decided it was the most sensible thing to do. They had both houses valued, their solicitors drew up contracts and deposits were paid on exchange of contract. On completion, my friend only had to pay the difference in the value of the two houses plus her stamp duty. Here's how it could work:

> A has a house worth £140,000.
> B has a house worth £165,000.
> They swap properties.
> A has to pay £25,000 to B plus £1,650 stamp duty.

Apparently, this is happening quite a lot in post-divorce cases with the necessary downsizing. The real financial advantages are that you save on estate agent's commission and the stamp duty only has to be paid on one property (the higher value property), since a change in legislation. Searches still have to be carried out and proper contracts drawn up so that the swap is a fully legal transaction, but you could end up saving yourself thousands of pounds.

Estate agents

Whether you like it or not, not all estate agents are avaricious, smarmy, knobbly-kneed sharks! They want to sell you a property come hell or high water, so it is up to you to sort the wheat from the chaff. You could telephone several estate agents in your targeted area and get them to send you details of available properties. Be specific about your budget and needs and explain, firmly, that you cannot afford the time to see unsuitable properties, as they will often try to persuade you to see something that is way over your budget. Let your fingers do the walking. You will be sent all sorts of details, most of which will be highly unsuitable. Don't get frustrated, but if you think that the agent simply isn't on your wavelength, go elsewhere.

It may be worth registering with several agents in the area. Ring to book an appointment first to show that you are serious about buying. Ask your friends for a personal recommendation, but if they can't come up with anything, you could always try the National Association of Estate Agents. (See Useful Addresses.) Different agents deal in different types of property, so it would be wise to spend a moment looking at the sort of properties they have advertised in their windows. Some agents only deal with a certain section of the market.

I have always found that going into an estate agent's office in person can reap rewards. You are no longer a faceless number on their records but a real person with clear ideas about what you want. Developing a professional friendship with an agent has meant that I am telephoned with information about a property that has just come on to the market, before they have even printed the details. This will help you if you find that every property in which you show an interest is already 'under offer'. Therefore, I am afraid you are going to have to show your face! Also be very charming on the phone – a little schmoozing goes a long way!

Make your agents work for their money by contacting them regularly for updates on what has come on to the market. Let them know that you have been given a 'decision in principle' from your lender meaning you are in a position to move swiftly once an offer has been accepted. This will give you the edge over another buyer who may be waiting to sell their property. If time is of the essence, don't bother to see anything that is already under offer. It could be a complete waste of time.

As a first-time buyer making your first tentative steps on to the property market, you are in a strong position as far as the estate agent is concerned, because you have nothing to sell and therefore can break the chain. However, you must have all your finances in order so that the agent takes you seriously as a potential buyer.

If you are selling a property it is wise to give the impression that your home is already under offer, otherwise the agent might not take you seriously. Most people say that looking at properties to buy before you have sold your own home (by that, I mean, have exchanged contracts) will lead to heartbreak. The number of times I have heard sob stories from friends who have found their dream home, only to be pipped at the post by someone with the money in their pocket. The moral of this story is: make sure your home has a firm offer before you start to look around.

CHECKLIST

Checklist for dealing with estate agents

Check the local newspapers. ☐

Jot down numbers on For Sale boards. ☐

Use the internet. ☐

Read the ads in national newspapers. ☐

Try the auctions. ☐

Telephone local agents with your brief. ☐

Look in estate agents' windows. ☐

Check the glossy magazines. ☐

Check the private ads. ☐

Make friends with your chosen agent and be persistent. ☐

Let your fingers do the walking. ☐

Be selective. ☐

Never view without an agent or friend (if you are female). ☐

Understanding floor plans, details and photos

Once you have received all your information and property details from all those various sources, you will need to weed them out. Poor you! I remember being totally overwhelmed by the stuff arriving through the letterbox each morning, but it's easy to play property sleuth when you know how.

Details

First, stick to your original brief. You have arrived at a property specification that meets your minimum requirements and a budget that takes into account all the extra costs, so don't be swayed by anything else. This will waste time. Bin all the details that look tempting but cost too much. Going to visit houses that you can't afford is fine if you are aspirational or voyeuristic, but it just wastes everyone's time and leaves you feeling inadequate. If you need three bedrooms, don't look at anything with fewer than three. Read the details carefully. These days estate agents' details are a lot more honest than they used to be, thanks to the Misdescriptions Act, but there are still words to be wary of.

Individual is one. 'Decorated in a very individual style' means that no one else likes it!

Double glazing means constant traffic noise.

Store room/bedroom 3 probably means the bedroom is the size of a shoebox.

In need of modernisation is another beauty. Probably means it is about to fall down.

Bijou: can't swing a cat.

Reduced for quick sale: still overpriced.

Mature garden: overgrown jungle.

Potential: if you've got loads of money.

School close by: children play in your front garden.

Spacious: too big to heat.

Full of character: full of woodworm.

Floor plans

Floor plans are becoming increasingly important and some people would rather see a good floor plan than pictures. I am a huge fan of the floor plan because it can tell you far more than words can about the layout of the property. For example, if it says 'from hallway through into a large open sitting room', which way did I turn, left or right? With a floor plan you can see exactly the location of the sitting room off the hallway, and you can also see where the windows and fireplaces are, and the geography of the bedrooms and bathroom. If you have children, things like this are very important.

When we first saw the details of our house, it was the floor plan that sold it to us, not the photographs or the words or the history. It met all the basic criteria I had for moving to a house in the country. This is why you must be absolutely clear on what it is you need to buy.

Photographs

Photographs should only be viewed as a guideline and are often misleading. If you are buying a Victorian terraced property then the house is, presumably, the same as the one next door. They are used as the emotional key to pull you through the door. 'If there's only one photograph on the details, it's got to be good one, otherwise the purchaser isn't grabbed,' said one estate agent. He admitted that sometimes they have to go back to rephotograph a property if the original shot isn't doing the trick.

Of course the internet is making life much easier for the foreign investor but with photographs they've got it down to a fine art. They only take exterior pictures at certain months of the year, when the garden looks perfect and the sky is the clearest blue. Like the wording, photographs can be economical with the truth. They say the camera never lies? Oh yes it does! So don't be taken in.

Don't be tempted to go miles out of your way to see a property that looks wonderful, fits your criteria and seems much cheaper than everything else in the area. There has to be a catch. So start asking questions.

Questions to ask the estate agent before you decide to view

Call the agent and put him on the spot. 'Before I view, can I ask you a few questions? No. 4 The Grove seems a very good price. Why is that?' *'Well actually it's near a busy main road.'* 'Oh, what about 35 Acacia Avenue, that looks so smart?' *It's lovely but it's next to a fish-and-chip shop.* 'What about Oxford House? That seems perfect for us, but why is it so cheap?' *Well, it is very spacious but some people are put off by the fact that there is an industrial estate on the doorstep.*

Believe me, if you ask enough questions you will save yourself an awful lot of viewings. The agent has to be honest if you ask direct questions. When we were looking for our house, I was very taken with one house in Northamptonshire. It seemed perfect for us, so we went to have a look, without me grilling the agent first. Big mistake.

The house was lovely. Except it had a public footpath 10 ft from the front door going right along the edge of the garden!

QUESTIONS TO ASK...YOUR ESTATE AGENT BEFORE YOU VIEW A PROPERTY

Q Is it realistically priced?

Q Where is the nearest railway station?

Q How far is the main road?

Q What is directly opposite/next to the property?

Q Can you hear the motorway?

Q How big is the garden?

Q How far are the shops?

Q What are the neighbours like?

Q Where is the nearest school?

Q What are the service charges?

Q What council tax band is it in?

Q How much are the quarterly gas and electricity bills?

Q Are there any current disputes involving rights of way or fences or trees?

Q How long has it been on the market?

Q How long is the lease?

Q Why are the current occupants moving?

Viewing a property and how to do it

Be prepared to take your time when viewing. This is a crucial decision you are about to make. When I buy a property I view it not once or twice, but three or four times, sometimes more. This is because the property will take on a different character at different times of the day. Depending which way it is facing, some rooms may be really gloomy when you want them to be brightest. If you have received details of a property that looks really nice and after you have asked all the relevant questions, make an appointment to view it immediately. You can't afford to hang around procrastinating because you'll never snap up a bargain that way. Time is of the essence. Sometimes the estate agent will accompany you to the viewing, particularly if the property is empty, and sometimes the owner will show you around instead. In my experience it is preferable to have the estate agent with you, as they tend to bend your ear far less than the owners do! It's amazing how even the most silent types become verbose when trying to sell a house.

Take a notebook, pen and tape measure with you so that you can check certain areas for the treasured piece of furniture that you want to bring with you. Also, taking notes will help you to remember certain details if you are viewing several properties in one day. For example, I always write down things like 'needs rewiring, bathrooms OK, kitchen horrible but tiles OK, sitting room too small etc.'

Try not to be put off by other people's taste (see page 28 for Spotting the Potential). Their choice of colours and furniture might not be to your liking so look beyond all that and try to envisage what the house will look like with your belongings in it. Similarly, an exquisitely decorated house with expensive furniture can be misleading because it gives the impression of luxury and style but could be a bad investment if it is in the wrong location.

Take your time and don't be rushed by the estate agent or the owner. This is a massive investment you are making so it is imperative that you get it right. Note down the height of the ceilings, the sunlight or lack of it in each room, the direction of the garden and the state of garden fencing etc.

Look out for any tell-tale patches of damp or dark staining on the ceiling, which could mean there is a leak above. If all the lights are on, turn them off and see how dark it is. Ask when the central heating boiler was last serviced. If you really like showers, turn the shower on to test the pressure. If it is a pathetic dribble you may need to install a pressure pump.

After the first viewing, and assuming you are really interested in the property, make arrangements with the agent or the seller to see it again after work. They want to sell it, so they won't mind. This will show you different things like how difficult it is to park your car after work and how noisy it is with the children back from school. If the seller is there, don't be afraid to ask lots of questions. (See page 66.)

The last question – why are you moving – can sometimes be very revealing. If they stammer and start waffling about it being 'time to move on' it probably means that they've had a row with the neighbours or the flight path is getting too much. Remember, most people move home for a reason, so you must do your research. Here are some more details to check out.

Things to look out for when viewing a property

Interior

- Is the layout all right?

- What is the condition of the structure?

- What is included in the price?

- Any cracks in the walls?

- Is the kitchen big enough?

- Are the windows double glazed?

- Any peeling wallpaper (due to damp)?

- Is there a utility room?

- Any condensation on windows?

- Condition of windows?

- Fresh paint – is that a cover-up?

- What storage is there?

- Springy floors – are the joists rotting?

- Woodworm or dry rot?

- Are there enough electrical sockets?

- Does it have a damp-proof course?

- Is the bathroom big enough?

- Is there sufficient water pressure?

Exterior

- What state is the garden in?

- Damaged or blocked guttering?

- The state of brickwork and rendering?

- Bulging or cracked walls?

- Damaged chimneys?

- Missing roof tiles?

- Is the drive in good condition?

- Is there a garage?

- Is there off-road parking?

- Are sheds and greenhouses included in the price?

- Is it on a steep slope?

- Is the garden south-facing and is it big enough?

- Are the drains OK?

Don't waste time viewing a property if you know within the first few minutes that you don't like it. Say to the agent or owner that it's not quite what you were looking for and they won't mind at all. It saves a lot of time and effort on their part.

Dos and Don'ts

- **Do** view the property as many times as you feel necessary.

- **Do** ask lots of questions.

- **Do** check the plumbing.

- **Do** take measurements if a beloved piece of furniture is coming with you.

- **Do** research the location and local facilities.

- **Do** get a survey (see page 109).

- **Do** trust your instincts.

- **Do** check that the price is competitive.

- **Do** take your time.

- **Don't** view anything that doesn't fit your basic brief.

- **Don't** believe everything the agent says.

- **Don't** be put off by a pushy seller.

- **Don't** be put off by the seller's ghastly choice of wallpaper!

- **Don't** be put off by a posh estate agent.

- **Don't** forget the costs of stamp duty, council tax, ground rent, service charges, etc.

CASE STUDY

The very first property that Jackie Holler viewed was immediately dismissed as being too small. She saw several other houses and it quickly became apparent that her budget was not going to stretch as far as she had hoped and that the first house wasn't small at all. By the time she requested a second viewing several weeks later – the house was under offer. It is important, therefore, to make comparisons quickly so that you know what you can get for your money and don't lose the property that you want.

Putting in an offer

Assuming you have found the home of your dreams – well, something that fits your basic criteria – you will need to make a formal offer. If the property is being handled by an estate agent you should ring them immediately and make an offer. Some people offer well below the asking price on principle thinking that they can get the property for a better price. Having done your research, only you will know if this is a good idea. If you feel that the property is realistically priced then I would go ahead and offer the asking price. No point in messing about.

If your offer is below the asking price the agent will put it to the seller and there will be a bit of negotiation until everyone is agreed on the price. This means your offer has been accepted but this should be 'subject to contract and survey'.

'Subject to contract' means that they will sell and you will buy it only if both parties are happy with the various contractual negotiations. After your survey you may decide not to buy it or to renegotiate the price.

The agent should then agree this in writing and will ask for your solicitor's details. If you do not already have a solicitor there are plenty of high street solicitors who specialise solely in conveyancing and who will do it for a fixed fee, plus disbursements, which will include the extra costs for searches, land registry, copy deeds etc. (See page 102 for more on Solicitors.)

It is important that you let the agent and the seller know that yours is a serious offer and that you intend to buy. You would be in a very strong position if:

- you have a mortgage certificate guaranteeing an offer of a loan;

- you already have a buyer for your home;

- you are a first-time buyer (no chain);

- you are a cash buyer.

How to negotiate

Every property has its price and unfortunately for you this will sometimes be way beyond your budget. However, due to market fluctuations some of those prices will be hugely inflated and, as we saw in the early 1990s, prices plummeted alarmingly making the unaffordable suddenly affordable. Negotiating on your dream home is not for the faint-hearted because, as I have said before, procrastination leads to disappointment. I tend not to negotiate very much on an emotional purchase (i.e. my home), but get very tough on an investment. Therefore, ask yourself whether this is a temporary investment home with a view to a profit, or is this to be your family home for years to come.

Ask yourself the following questions to help you decide whether you are willing to pay the asking price or make a lower offer.

- How much can you afford to pay?

- How many other buyers are after the same house? (If there are several it will give you less room for bargaining.)

- How does the price compare with similar properties in the area?

- How much do you want the house and are you prepared to pay over the odds for it?

Once you have made your offer the estate agent will put it to the owner/owners and you may have to wait a while before getting a response. If it has only been on the market for a week, the seller is more likely to bide his time than if it has been on the market for six months. This is when you must let them know that you are serious and have all your finances in order.

- Have you made it clear that your offer is subject to contract and survey?

- Have you asked the estate agent:
  to take the property off the market?
  whether they are the sole agent?
  to make sure any other agents take it off the market too?

- If you are a first-time buyer, have you made this clear?

- Have you supplied the estate agent with your solicitor's details?

- Do you have all the documents and information you need to make your formal mortgage application?

- Are you prepared to leave a small deposit as a sign of good intent (some estate agents ask for this)?

- Are you putting them under pressure by suggesting a quick exchange?

- Have you booked a surveyor?

CASE STUDY

Mark and Sue Burns thought they had found their dream home and put in an offer of the asking price of £495,000. This was accepted and it was then agreed that the house would be taken off the market.

While waiting for the results of their survey Mark Burns got a call from the seller suggesting that they up their offer by another 5 per cent in order to get into a contract race and whoever was in a position to exchange contracts the quickest would get the house.

Mark was furious and didn't want to get into a race. He realised they had been gazumped and decided to pull out of the sale altogether. This was the right thing to do.

They were living in a rented house and, as time went by, finding nothing suitable to buy, Mark became very angry. The agent had, in his opinion, gone against the agreement and continued to show the property. Mark complained to the NAEA and the agent was found guilty of professional misconduct.

Remember you can negotiate the price of the property if you are on a stamp duty threshold. For example, if the property is £260,000 you will be faced with £7,500 of stamp duty instead of £2,500 if it were below the £250,000 threshold. There is no stamp duty payable on extras like carpets and curtains, so it is possible to pay £250,000 for the house and £10,000 for all the extras, but you must ask your solicitor to have this stated clearly in the contract. However, some solicitors don't like doing this as the Inland Revenue might get suspicious if you claim you paid £10,000 for a moth-eaten old rug, so be realistic.

TOP TIPS

Here are my eight top tips for staying sane.

1. Keep a cool head at all times.

2. Be patient.

3. Be persistent with the agent.

4. Be prepared to negotiate.

5. Try not to get emotionally involved (there will always be another house).

6. Ask lots of questions (your solicitor is there to help you).

7. Remember, the internet is a mine of information.

8. Keep taking the tablets!

CHAPTER 4

Buying your home

The procedure

Getting into a chain

Choosing a solicitor

Conveyancing

Surveys

Leasehold and freehold

Buying in Scotland

Final checklist for buying your home

There follows a step-by-step guide to the procedure involved in buying your home, from making an offer to completion.

Before you start thinking about the colour of your bedroom walls and sending out the house-warming invitations, these are the basic steps you need to take before you are given those much-wanted keys.

1. Arrange a mortgage.

2. Make an offer.

3. Give your solicitor's details to the estate agent.

4. Get a property valuation.

5. Organise a survey.

6. If happy with the survey, pay deposit and exchange contracts.

7. Set date for completion.

8. Make sure balance of money is ready for transfer.

9. Day of completion, receive keys.

10. Property is registered in your name.

The procedure

Once your offer has been accepted the wheels are really in motion. Assuming that your lender has given you a **decision in principle** they will probably want to do a **valuation of the property** to make sure that their percentage is secure. If you are borrowing 90 per cent of the total and the property is undervalued by the lender you may have a problem making up the shortfall.

Assuming all is well you should **arrange a survey** of the property before proceeding, for your own peace of mind. You do not want to invest in a home with chronic subsidence and rising damp. (See below, pages 109–15, for more on Surveys.)

The **surveyor's report** will tell you all sorts of things about the property, which, hopefully, are not too scary. If, however, it does highlight a serious problem such as subsidence, you may be able to negotiate the price down even further. If everything then is OK you will receive a long and boring list from the seller's solicitor listing all the **fixtures and fittings** that are going to stay and those that are not. Go through this carefully as you may be under the impression that certain things are being left, such as garden benches or light fittings.

When everything is agreed and your solicitor has done the **searches** (this is to make sure that there isn't a by-pass planned past your front door), has all the answers to his enquiries and has seen the title deeds (these outline the details of your property such as whether it is freehold or leasehold and any rights you will have over restrictions imposed on the property), he will then draw up a contract and you will need to **arrange a date for completion**. This is traditionally 28 days after **exchange of contract**. However, it can be brought forward or delayed to accommodate both parties. Exchange of contract is when you will need to get 10 per cent of the sale price to your solicitor so that he can pass it on to the seller's solicitor.

Then you can **exchange contracts**… Hurrah! You are now in a situation where you are legally bound to complete the sale of the property. If you decide to back out at this stage you will forfeit your deposit and could be sued by the owner for his losses for your breach of contract.

The good news is that the property is now as good as yours and no one can sneak in and take it from you (you can't get gazumped). The bad news is you now have to find the money to pay all that horrible stamp duty and legal fees etc.

As the **date of completion** approaches you can start making plans for the move (see Chapter 9). If you want to take measurements at the property or show your decorator around for a quote, gaining access should not be a problem. You have committed to buy the property after all, but some sellers can be quite emotional about this and don't want to let you in again until completion. Try sweet-talking them, or take round a bunch of flowers.

On the **day of completion** the property will be legally yours when the seller's solicitor has received the balance of the money. This is usually wired (sent by bank transfer) direct from your solicitor. You can then collect the keys.

Congratulations, you can now move in. **Post completion**, your solicitor will pay the stamp duty, register you as the new owner and send you his bill.

Before you exchange it is essential that:

- you have arranged your mortgage;

- you are on the point of exchanging on any property you are selling;

- you are happy with the survey;

- your solicitor has done all the searches;

- you have received all the answers to your pre-contract enquiries;

- there will be vacant possession;

- the building is covered by insurance.

Sealed bids

If there are several offers for the same property, the agents will suggest **sealed bids** instead of going to each individual party and asking them to up the price. This also prevents gazumping. If you find yourself in this situation you will be asked to put your offer – or bid – into an envelope. On the day of the sale the envelopes are opened by the estate agent and the property, rather like at auction, will go to the highest bidder. However, there is no way to guarantee success when buying property this way, unless you have very deep pockets and are prepared to put in a very high bid.

There are two kinds of sealed bid.

1. **Formal tender** – once the envelopes are opened and the bid is accepted, the sale is complete. There is no going back.

2. **Informal tender** – the sealed bid is subject to survey and contract. In other words, until you exchange contracts either party can pull out.

CASE STUDY

A famous actress of my acquaintance found a house in the West Country that she fell in love with as a second home. It was on the market for £395,000 and she offered the asking price immediately. The agents then went very quiet and stopped returning her calls. She simply wanted to find out whether her offer had been accepted and what the problem was, if any. Eventually, after several days, an agent called her back and said that there had been considerable interest in this house and asked whether she would be prepared to increase her offer. She said she definitely would and needed to know where the current offer stood. To her amazement the price had jumped to £500,000. She offered £510,000 and was then told that the agents were going to accept sealed bids. She rang me to ask my advice and I told her that if she wanted the house she was going to have to write down her ceiling price (as in an auction) or risk losing it. The bids were going to formal tender so she offered £560,000. The following day she rang me in tears. The house had gone for £610,000 and it transpired that there had been six people after the same property.

Now, this situation is unusual but does happen on the more desirable properties. You can only offer what *you* think it is worth.

Getting into a chain

Eek! This is so horrible and stressful I'm having palpitations just writing about it. I'm sure you all know about being in 'a chain', because even if you haven't been there yourself, we all know someone who has.

Being in a chain is when you are selling your house to someone who is buying your house only when he has sold his house to someone else who has to sell their house first and so on and so on. You may be trying to buy a house as well – have set your heart on it – but the sale is dependent on you selling first. Or even, you are buying but the seller won't move until he has found somewhere to buy.

Confused? Being in the middle of the chain is horrific and awful, and often the whole thing collapses because one buyer drops out, so you all have to wait until another buyer is found.

I have only been involved in a chain once and then I vowed never again. The problem is that most people want to sell and buy on the same day. Completion is synchronised so that you move out of one property and into another on that day. This is madness. It is totally dependent on your buyer coming up with the money in time for your solicitor to pass it on so that you can have the keys to your new home. This is why we hear stories of removal men sitting outside a house for hours on end, waiting to be let in, because the money has got stuck somewhere along the chain.

There are endless permutations and combinations of being in a chain, but there are also ways of avoiding it.

- Be a cash buyer. This means you are not dependent on selling a home and you don't need a loan (either you are very rich, have won the lottery or your granny just died).

- Sell your home first before you start looking to buy. Rent for the interim period and then when you see something you like you can move swiftly. Speed always strikes a mean deal. Estate agents always favour the buyer who doesn't have somewhere to sell or who is a cash buyer.

- Being a first-time buyer (this will put you at the end of the chain).

- Buy a brand-new home with no previous owner.

- Buy at auction.

- Sell at auction.

- Buy a property with 'vacant possession'. (The owner has already gone.)

- Sell your home to a cash buyer.

TOP TIPS

Here are my ten top tips for first-time buyers.

1. Always arrange your finances first before you start looking.

2. Get to know an area.

3. Look out for transport links.

4. Check out the local facilities.

5. Time your journey to work.

6. Shop around for a good estate agent.

7. Be specific about your needs.

8. Visit the local pubs and restaurants to see if you like the area.

9. What kind of people live there already?

10. Find yourself a good solicitor – preferably through a personal recommendation.

Choosing a solicitor

In my opinion a personal recommendation for a solicitor is preferable to walking in cold but if none of your friends can help, it is fairly easy to find a solicitor who can do your conveyancing. There are high street solicitors (ask your estate agent or mortgage broker), the local newspapers will carry advertisements for specialists in conveyancing or you could call the Law Society (see Useful Addresses),which will provide you with a list of solicitors in your area.

The term 'conveyancing' literally means that the property will be conveyed or transferred from one party to another.

Most conveyancing is done on a fixed minimum fee plus disbursements (any extras, such as Land Registry fees and searches) plus VAT. The conveyancing fee is usually based on the value of your property, as is the Land Registry fee (see page 37).

Fees for conveyancing work can vary enormously, so try to get at least three quotes over the telephone from different firms, and ask them what is included in their quote. For most firms this is fairly standard but it should include:

- charges for the solicitor's time;

- solicitor's indemnity fee, all phone calls and letters (any overseas phone calls will be charged extra);

- the lender's legal work;

- drawing up a mortgage deed;

- the report on title;

- drawing up the lease (leasehold properties require more work);

- checking on service charges (if any);

- dealing with seller's solicitor;

- local authority search fees;

- paying stamp duty;

- Land Registry fees (registering the property).

> Make sure you choose a solicitor who specialises in residential conveyancing and not criminal law. Don't choose someone who may be good at representing burglars but rubbish at buying houses.

If you are selling a home it would make sense to use the same solicitor for both the house you are selling and the one you are buying.

Having chosen your solicitor, there are a few things you will need to take with you when you first meet him or her:

- some form of ID;

- your mortgage lender's details;

- your cheque book.

No two conveyancing transactions are alike and complications can arise to do with boundaries or the lease, which is why you are paying a professional to deal with the process.

Your solicitor will also make some local authority searches to find out if there are proposed plans for the area. For example, are they planning a by-pass in the area or is a housing estate about to be built opposite your property? Are you buying in a conservation area so that future building may be restricted? Your solicitor will also complete searches at the Land Registry that will provide further information about the property.

A solicitor who drags his feet can make life extremely stressful for you, so before instructing him make sure you get a timescale of the proceedings to exchange and completion. Keep in regular contact to maintain the momentum.

Licensed conveyancers

There is an alternative to using a solicitor and that is a licensed conveyancer who, unlike solicitors, concentrates solely on dealing with property transactions and can handle the purchase, sale and mortgage of freehold/leasehold properties. They are regulated by the Council for Licensed Conveyancers (see Useful Addresses) and must provide insurance and compensation to protect the client. However, if you need other legal services to be provided, such as making a will, you would be advised to deal with a solicitor.

QUESTIONS TO ASK... YOUR SOLICITOR

Don't pretend that you understand what your solicitor is saying, if you don't. I always tend to plead ignorance and have things spelt out in words of one syllable, rather than be caught on the hop when it is time to exchange. Here are a few questions that it might be worth asking.

Q Are they a member of the Law Society?

Q Do they specialise in conveyancing?

Q Do they have a complaints procedure?

Q What are their rates?

Q What is included in their quote?

Q What are the extra charges likely to be (i.e. searches, Land Registry, copy deeds)?

Q What is the timescale? (If you're in a hurry you will need to know how soon they can start on your conveyancing.)

Q What will you have to pay upfront?

List of key words solicitors might use

Vendor The seller of the property.

Caveat emptor Latin for 'let the buyer beware'.

CCJ County Court Judgment.

Lessee Is the holder of the lease.

Lessor Is a person who lets property on a lease, otherwise known as the freeholder.

Freeholder The person who owns the freehold.

Equity The value of the property minus the mortgage loan left to pay. ▶

Negative equity The sum of your loan exceeds the value of your property.

Title deeds Legal ownership documents for a property.

Reddendum The part of the lease that defines what ground rent is payable and when.

Gazumping When a potential buyer is outbid by a rival buyer.

Gazundering When the buyer informs the seller that he will only proceed if the price is reduced.

Guarantor Someone who promises to pay your mortgage repayments if you default on them.

Covenant A promise made by previous owners that certain things would not be done on the land, such as demolishing a barn or changing a pathway.

Easement A right for someone to do something on your land such as walking across it to gain access to their property or the right to have light coming into their property.

Conveyancing

Once you have put in your offer and it has been accepted, and assuming the survey is satisfactory, your solicitor will leap into action to get you to the next stage, which is exchange of contracts. The seller's solicitor will prepare a pre-contract package, which will consist of copies of the draft contract, proof of seller's ownership and a seller's property information form (SPIF). This will also include a fixtures, fittings and contents form showing what is included and what is excluded from the purchase price. This pre-contract package isn't law yet but most solicitors use it to speed things along. It may also include some land searches that have already been investigated, which give additional information regarding the property.

The buyer's solicitor must follow a number of procedures. First, they must make sure that the terms of the draft contract are in accordance with the buyer's wishes. The contract is a standard document including all the information essential for the purchase of the property, i.e. details of the property, address, purchase price, deposit, date for completion, name and address of both seller and buyer, plus any rights that third parties have over the property, which could include covenants, or an easement.

After completing local authority searches and searches at the Land Registry, your solicitor will be ready to exchange contracts with the seller's solicitor.

When everyone is happy you will be asked to sign the contract and then hand over the agreed deposit. Both parties sign separate copies of the same contract, which are then exchanged and a date agreed for completion. Up until the point of actually exchanging contracts, you can pull out of the proceedings without incurring any penalty. Once you have exchanged, there is no going back.

The final part of the solicitor's job is to arrange the completion of the sale – the finalising of the deal. One important point for the solicitor to check before completion is that the buyer's mortgage arrangement is satisfactory, the money is standing by and the client is happy with the conditions.

You have completed on the property when:

- the terms agreed in the contract have been included in the final transfer deed;

- the buyer's funds have been transferred from the lender to the seller's account;

- the buyer can now have the keys to the property: hurrah!

After completion the solicitor registers the transfer deed with the Land Registry. Until this is done, the buyer will not have legal ownership of the property. The deeds are then sent to the lender, or , if you have bought without borrowing any money, can be sent to you or left for safekeeping with your solicitor. Your solicitor should provide you with a copy of the Land Certificate, showing you as the 'registered proprietor'.

Do-it-yourself conveyancing

Only the extremely brave or those with a knowledge of the law should undertake their own conveyancing. It is extremely complicated and time-consuming, and if you are getting a mortgage you may not be saving very much money as you'll still have to pay the fees for the lender's solicitor.

If you are selling a home and buying at the same time, surely this is stressful enough without taking on the legal work. You will need to get hold of several forms; put aside a lot of time during office hours and be familiar with the legal protocol.

I strongly recommend using a solicitor to do your conveyancing, especially if your property is any of the following:

- not freehold or not registered;
- being sold at auction;
- being sold as new by a builder;
- not a house;
- part of a house;
- being sold by a couple who are getting divorced;
- not in England or Wales;
- has a sitting tenant;
- being sold privately.

Surveys

Only 20 per cent of homebuyers currently bother with a survey. This is total madness to me, because how on earth can you know what horrors are lurking beneath the floorboards, unless an expert tells you? As a major financial investment it seems sensible to inspect the goods first. You wouldn't buy a car without checking for dodgy brakes, would you?

Why surveys are so important

Although the lender will have already organised a valuation survey to be carried out, it is advisable to hire the expertise of a chartered surveyor to report on the condition of the property. A valuation survey simply takes into account the estimated value of the property, but does not take a specific look at the condition of the various aspects of the building. (Ask your lender what their valuation fee will be – some will waive it completely.) A proper survey will highlight areas of the building that need attention. This is crucial information as it not only makes you aware of what you are committing yourself to, it can also give you some leverage in reducing the asking price as well. Although it is yet another expense, it is one you ignore at your peril.

The different types of survey

The homebuyer's report

The most basic survey is known as the Homebuyer's Report. Every element of the building is considered. However, it is important to note that this appraisal is made by simply looking and assessing, and no extensive tests are carried out. Most people opt for this type of survey because it is the least expensive, but it is only really recommended for relatively new houses, i.e. those built in the last 30 years. The report will normally include a valuation and an insurance valuation.

This type of survey will help you to make an informed judgement on whether or not you still want to buy the property. It will also help you decide whether or not the agreed price is fair.

They normally cost between £250-£350 for an average size house, but this obviously depends on the area.

Building survey

This is a more detailed survey that should be recommended for any house that predates the Second World War. This is generally the most favoured type of survey as the surveyor will give a fuller explanation. The building is examined carefully and the surveyor will then produce a written report on his findings. As with the Homebuyer's Report there will be a list of caveats – areas that have not been examined, such as drains and foundations. This is perfectly normal, but it is important to look through these omissions and make sure that you are happy to exclude them. No valuation figure will normally be given unless specifically asked for.

This type of survey is usually tailored to your individual requirements, particularly if you are concerned about an area within the property.

Costs vary enormously, but will be from £400 upwards, depending on the size of the property and the area, and it can take up to 14 days before you receive the report.

Full structural survey

This is the most expensive survey available, but it is essential if the house you are buying is clearly in very poor condition, is

If the vendor has had any work done on the house in the past to improve its condition such as a damp-proof course, woodworm or dry rot treatment, there should be a guarantee with the improvements and your solicitor should ask for verification. Any special treatments will have a guarantee lasting approximately 20 years.

extremely old or has had a lot of alterations. This report is similar to the Building Condition Survey but there are no caveats, everything is checked and areas of the house will be opened up for extensive inspection and testing. This survey may be the most expensive (costs vary, depending on the state of your property), but it will definitely give you peace of mind. Again, it will not include a valuation unless asked for. These surveys can take anything from 7 to 20 days to be completed.

Before you seek the help of a surveyor here are some important things to think about:

• always ask beforehand how much the survey will cost;

• ask the surveyor to recommend which kind of report is suitable to the prospective property;

• ask the surveyor to estimate the cost of repairs in the report;

• check that your surveyor is part of the Royal Institute for Chartered Surveyors (RICS). They are assessed yearly on their performance, have regular training updates and are insured.

How to choose a surveyor

Once you have decided which report you require you will need to find a surveyor. I always think a personal recommendation is best so ask a friend who has just bought a property. Otherwise, your lender or solicitor should be able to come up with a few names. (I'm sceptical about asking the agent for a surveyor, in case the agent is biased.)

The Royal Institute of Chartered Surveyors is a regulatory body that represents thousands of surveyors, so they could recommend somebody in your area. (See Useful Addresses). It's wise to use a local surveyor as he'll need to do less research on the area, which will speed up the process a bit. Also make sure he specialises in your type of house if it is in a particularly unusual category, such as a Jacobean timber frame house or a thatched cottage.

QUESTIONS TO ASK... YOUR SURVEYOR

Q Are you a qualified member of the RICS (Royal Institute of Chartered Surveyors)?

Q Are you locally based?

Q Which sort of report do I need?

Q How long will it take?

Q How soon can you do it?

Q When can I see it?

Q What will you be looking for?

Q Can you carry out the valuation as well?

Q Will you estimate the cost of repairs in the report?

Q Will you be prepared to explain it and talk me through it?

Q Are you married? (This is for all you Bridget Jones types.)

Q And, most importantly, how much will it cost?

Ask your surveyor to organise an electrical, plumbing and heating survey from suitably qualified firms if it is thought advisable. Asbestos cladding and insulation can be a very expensive problem with pre-1970 houses. Do not forget that once you have exchanged contracts, it is too late to renegotiate the price.

Understanding your survey

Don't worry if it all seems confusing. After you have read it really carefully, call your surveyor and ask him to explain the bits you don't understand. If he recommends that certain things are done *before* you exchange contracts, make sure the seller is made aware as soon as possible. This may give you room to negotiate on the price. Also, if there is a legal problem made apparent in the survey (a public footpath has suddenly appeared), talk to your solicitor immediately.

Remember:

- a valuation from your lender is not a survey;

- your surveyor should be local and a member of the RICS;

- there are basically two types of survey – the Homebuyer's Report and the Building Survey;

- if your home is brand new, make sure it has the NHBC warranty (see below);

- you can withdraw your offer if the survey reveals serious problems or negotiate on the price;

- make sure planning permission was given for any extensions or alterations;

- always budget for more than one survey, in case your offer is bettered.

A NEWLY BUILT HOME

The National House Building Council (NHBC) is the independent regulator and standard setter for the new homes industry in the UK (see Useful Addresses). They have 18,000 house builders registered with them who are put through a technical and financial vetting system. Builders must comply with NHBC Rules and Standards or risk investigation.

The NHBC provides a ten-year Buildmark Cover Warranty on the structure of a new house, and a range of warranty and insurance services for conversions, community housing and self-build projects. For the first two years after your home is completed it is up to the builder to put things right and for the remaining eight years you are covered by the NHBC in respect of major structural defects.

Some jargon busters

Urgent repairs: for example subsidence or some dodgy chimney stacks. These defects are judged to be a developing threat to the building or to personal safety. These should be put right as soon as possible and may affect your decision to buy. Obtain quotes for required work where appropriate.

Significant matters requiring further investigation, for example, suspected subsidence. These defects may affect the price you are willing to pay. You should get (and may have to pay for) reports and quotes from various builders.

Significant but not urgent repairs and renewals, could mean the need for a new covering for the garage roof in a few months' time.

A potential source of trouble, such as the building's vulnerable location near some water meadows, to which the surveyor is drawing your attention.

Legal matters, could mean a public footpath, which you should instruct your legal advisers to include in their preliminary enquiries.

The Law Society's TransAction Protocol

This Law Society scheme is used by many solicitors. The seller's solicitor determines whether it is used. If it is used, the seller's solicitor provides a package containing the following:

the draft contract;

copies of earlier title deeds (if unregistered) or official copies of the entries in the register (if registered);

a special form of preliminary enquiries called the property information form;

a fixtures, fittings and contents form, listing all the fixtures and fittings which are included in the price and those that will be removed by the seller. The idea behind the scheme is to get the paperwork under way quickly at the beginning of the transaction.

Fixtures and fittings

This is often an area causing dispute and upset, particularly on completion day when you finally get the keys, only to discover that all the door handles have been removed along with the bathroom mirror.

I heard about a chap who bought a house and found all the fireplaces had been ripped out and all the light fittings removed. In order to prevent this happening, it would be wise to get a list from the seller of all the things that are being left behind. The obvious ones are items that are *not* deemed to be moveable, such as:

- the garden shed;

- fireplaces;

- any wood panelling;

- light sockets;

- radiators or other forms of heating;

- water heaters or boiler;

- trees and shrubs in the garden;

- roof slates; and

- anything built-in or fitted.

The items that should be specified as either staying or going should include:

- the carpets and curtains;

- cooker/oven;

- fridge-freezer;

- washing machine, tumble drier and dishwasher;

- any light fittings;

- heaters or gas fires;

- lampshades or uplighters;

- garden benches, sheds, pots, swings etc.;

- bookshelves;

- curtain poles or tracks;

- bathroom fittings;

- any fancy door furniture;

- TV aerial etc.

When you receive the seller's list, if there is any uncertainty or confusion, ask the owner to go round the property with you, making another list. This way you can agree what stays and if there are items that the owner feels have an intrinsic value, you could make a separate offer for them.

I once bought a flat lock, stock and barrel with everything in it from beds to teaspoons, because the owner wanted to cash in his investment when the rental market bombed. This proved a fairly costly exercise, because once the tenant had moved out and I could get a really good look at everything, I discovered it was all pretty ghastly and would have to go. Be careful if tempted to do the same and remember you won't have to pay stamp duty on the contents.

Alternatively, you may be sent a really detailed **fixtures and fittings form** from the seller's solicitor, which the seller will have completed. It lists everything from ovens to curtain tracks and has three separate columns stating 'included', 'not included' and 'not applicable', which will make absolutely clear what is being taken and what is being left behind. This is part of the contract and is legally binding on the seller, so if he removes anything he's not supposed to, you will have a legal right to complain. *Tell your solicitor immediately.* This is part of the Law Society's Trans-Action Protocol (see page 115).

CASE STUDY

When I was selling a house years ago, the buyer expressed an interest in buying several items of furniture, as well as curtains and rugs etc. So we drew up a list of things he wanted and I put a price on them, based on what I thought they would fetch at auction. I had wanted to take the curtains with me to use at the next house but sometimes these are included in the price of a property and the agent's details will specify 'to include carpets, curtains and all fixtures'. Mine were *not* included.

After much negotiation, I decided not to sell any furniture to him because he was being unreasonable about the prices. The contracts were on the verge of being exchanged when he announced, through his solicitor, that he would not proceed unless I lowered the price of the house by £7,000 or included *all* the curtains. This is known as **gazundering** and usually only happens in a falling market.

I had filled in my fixtures and fittings list, which quite clearly stated that the curtains were not to be included, but my solicitor said the decision was mine. Either I tell the buyer to 'naff off' and put the house back on the market and start all over again or I agree to his demand. Which I did. My one proviso was that he exchange and complete by a certain date or I would withdraw the house. A horrid situation.

Leasehold and freehold

Extending the lease

If the property you want to buy has a short lease (and most mortgage companies won't lend on anything less than 64 years), it will be possible to extend the lease by applying to the freeholder.

This can be a fairly expensive procedure, as you will need a surveyor to carry out the valuation, and your solicitor will have to do extra paperwork, but you could try to share the cost of the extension with the freeholder.

Basically, to extend the lease, the property is valued at its current market value with its short lease and then given another valuation as if it were to have a 99-year lease. The difference is usually divided between the freeholder and leaseholder.

The obvious advantages of doing this are that it will make your property much more marketable when it is time to sell.

Buying the freehold

Occasionally on a leasehold property the freehold is offered for sale to be shared equally among the various leaseholders. In order to proceed you need collectively to appoint a solicitor to act on your behalf. The freehold must be purchased by 'one body' and in order to do that you will need to form a company that can act as the 'nominee purchaser'. It can be called Acacia Avenue Ltd or whatever the address is!

Even though the freehold can be acquired for a fairly reasonable amount each, being shared proportionally, this is exclusive of costs including solicitor's and landlord's fees, which may run into thousands, but once you have the freehold it will make your property more attractive.

The only recurring problem with sharing the freehold is that some owners like to manage the block between themselves instead of employing a managing agent, which can seem an unnecessary expense. This can lead to a breakdown between the freeholders if one or two of them decide not to pay their share of important repairs or buildings insurance.

Therefore:

- good managing agents act as mediators between flat owners and can insist on repairs and payments;

- make sure your managing agent is a member of the Association of Residential Managing Agents.

LEASEHOLD REFORM, HOUSING AND URBAN DEVELOPMENT ACT 1993

This Act has enabled leaseholders to buy their freeholds collect-ively, and individuals to extend their leases by 90 years. However there are strict rules as to residence (you have to have lived in the property for three years), and the procedures can be lengthy and the cost uncertain. It is essential to take advice from a solicitor or an agent who specialises in this field.

A few years ago I was offered a share of the freehold on my flat in a Victorian house in Kensington, West London. There were only four leaseholders in the house and we all thought it a very good idea indeed. The main benefit is that you can take control of the running of the house, will no longer have to pay ground rent and can appoint your own managing agents to take care of it. Also, owning a **shared freehold property** can be a lot more desirable when it is time to sell, since there is no limited timescale as there is with a lease.

In 1987 the **Landlord and Tenant Act** stated that if a non-resident freeholder wished to dispose of his property he must first give the leaseholders the opportunity to club together to buy the freehold. This is called the Right of First Refusal – but they weren't prosecuted if they ignored it. However, on 1 October 1996 when the Housing Act came into effect, they could be fined up to £2,500 for not explaining tenants' rights and another £5,000 if they sell the property despite those rights. So don't let anyone sell your freehold without consulting you first. It could be worth buying.

Commonhold and Leasehold Reform Bill

When this Bill becomes law it will create a new type of ownership called 'commonhold', which will eventually replace freehold. The main advantages would be that there would be no freeholder/landlord and that flat owners would share ownership of the land and the building, and be responsible for the maintenance of the property.

It will also be possible for leaseholders who do *not* take over the freehold to manage the property themselves instead of being dictated to by the management company. They would be responsible for all maintenance, management and collecting of service charges.

Just as a reminder, service charges include:

• the cleaning of the common parts;

• the maintenance of any lifts;

• the entry-phone;   ▶

- the porters' (if any) salaries;
- pest control;
- buildings insurance;
- the lighting of communal parts;
- general maintenance;
- sinking fund in case of major works.

Buying in Scotland

There are several major differences between Scottish and English law, and this becomes particularly apparent when buying or selling a property.

For example, there is no such thing as freehold or leasehold in Scotland as most buildings are owned on **feudal tenure**, which means that they are owned outright and can be sold freely in much the same way as freehold property in England.

However, the original landowner or developer is known as the **superior** and he can impose certain conditions on the future use of the property or land, a bit like a restrictive covenant. His consent will be required for any changes of use.

Flats do not have leases and are owned, like houses, on feudal tenure. The title deeds usually set out the way the various owners pay for maintenance of the building and shared responsibility of the external walls.

Finding your property

Solicitors often call themselves 'Solicitors *and Estate Agents*', because more properties are sold by solicitors than agents. There are solicitors' property centres in most of the major towns where you can see thousands of properties for sale. You will be given details and photographs of the property and the name of the solicitor who is selling it.

There are estate agents too, who work in the same way as those in England and Wales, so if you found a house you liked, you would need to instruct a solicitor in the normal way. The advantage of the property centres or solicitors' property department is that everything is under one roof.

Most property is for sale at 'offers over' a stated figure. This is sometimes known as the **upset price**, meaning the very minimum that the seller will consider accepting. Depending on the desirability of the property, it may well go for much more than the upset price.

Alternatively, houses are offered at a **fixed price** in order to get a quick sale. The first suitable offer at that price will secure the house.

You will need to instruct a solicitor to do your conveyancing fairly early on as things can progress very quickly. Make sure you get several quotes, as there are no fixed fees. Then your loan should be agreed so that you can move swiftly when you find your home. Securing a mortgage is the same as elsewhere in the UK.

When you have found the property that you like, you should tell your solicitor and he can deal with the seller's solicitor and do any negotiating on price or fixtures and fittings. The completion date, or **date of entry**, should also be discussed. At this stage, nothing is in writing and no formal offer has been made.

The procedure

The survey is the next step, **before** you make the offer, and is usually required by the banks or building societies before they will agree to the loan. The types of survey are similar to the rest of the UK (see page 109).

Once the surveyor's report has been returned and assuming there are no problems, you will be in a position to make an offer. The biggest difference when buying in Scotland is that this **offer is a formal document** and is legally binding, whereas in the rest of the UK a buyer can make several verbal offers on different properties, without any commitment, so it can be difficult for the seller to know if it is a serious offer.

The written document will state any conditions you have, any extras you may want to buy, the date you wish to move in and, finally, the price you are prepared to pay. Your solicitor will usually guide you as to how much over the upset price you should offer, but if more than one person is making an offer on the property, it becomes a bit of a risk – not unlike sealed bids (see page 98) – where you could be pipped by a higher offer. All offers will be requested on a certain date at a certain time. If unsuccessful it will cost you surveyor's fees and legal fees.

If, however, yours is the only offer and the date of entry is acceptable to the seller, the remaining legal matters are taken care of, such as planning proposals, searches or change of use if you wish to use part of the property as an office, for example.

Your offer will be subject to all these things and should any undesirable matters be disclosed, you can withdraw it or renegotiate the price. Stamp duty is payable, so a saving could be made if you allocate part of the price on to extras such as carpets and curtains.

If everyone is happy, your solicitor will send a letter to the seller's solicitor confirming that a binding contract is now concluded. The offer and all other subsequent letters between the solicitors are known as the **missives** and once they are concluded your solicitor will begin the process of transferring the property to you. This legal document when drawn up is known as the **disposition**.

Your solicitor will arrange for your loan to be made available by the date of entry and will ask you to sign the documents by that date. The difference between the loan and the price of the house will also have to be available on that date (if you are selling a house for example).

Once the full price of the property has been paid to the seller's solicitor, your solicitor will receive the title deeds, including the disposition, and you will be given the keys.

He will then register the disposition and send you the bill!

As solicitors in Scotland do not have a system of fixed fees here is what he will charge for:

- his time working up to the missives;

- the conveyancing and mortgage arrangements;

- registration fees;

- stamp duty

> £0–£60,000 is 0
> £60,001–£250,000 is 1%
> £250,001–£500,000 is 1.5%
> £500,000 and above is 2%;

- plus any extras such as bank charges or the copying of documents.

Here is a summary of the major differences you will encounter when buying a property in Scotland.

- In Scotland solicitors can act as estate agents, advertising property in local and national newspapers. They have offices that look like estate agents', but also have the staff to deal with the conveyancing and legal problems.

- The advantage is that the buyer only has one person to deal with.

- Solicitors can carry out their searches and enquiries very quickly because all properties are registered with a central land register, saving much time.

- The survey is done before you make an offer, and most property is freehold.

- Houses are advertised at a 'fixed price' or 'offers over' a certain price. You can't offer below.

- If the survey is satisfactory and you have arranged your finances with the lender, you can make the offer.

- The offer is made to the seller's solicitor and is legally binding once it has been accepted.

- These documents are known as missives and will include the date of entry, which is the date you wish to take possession of your home.

- Once the missives have been concluded, your solicitor will be sent the title deeds of the property.

- If everything is OK and searches turn up nothing too alarming, a document called the disposition will be drawn up, transferring the property to you.

- You give your solicitor the money and he arranges for the whole purchase price, including any mortgage, to be transferred to the seller's solicitor.

- You receive the keys on the date of entry, along with the disposition.

FINAL CHECK LIST FOR BUYING YOUR HOME

To finish off Part One of this book, here is a checklist covering all aspects of buying your home.

Where to live

Where are you going to live? ☐

Have you done your sums? ☐

What do you need to be comfortable? ☐

Are you starting a family? ☐

What do you need to be close to in the area? ☐

Have you checked the estate agents' windows? ☐

Have you checked the internet, newspapers etc.? ☐

Have you identified an up-and-coming area? ☐

If you are relocating, have you spent time there? ☐

Have you visited your chosen area at different times of the day? ☐

The money

Have you arranged your finance? ☐

Are you shopping around to compare deals? ☐

Are you checking the internet? ☐

Have you spoken to an IFA? ☐

Have you decided on repayment or endowment? ☐

Have you asked about arrangement fees, penalties, insurance policies, interest payments? ☐

Have you remembered the extra costs such as stamp duty, legal fees, survey, the deposit, moving costs and insurance? ☐

The agent

Have you found a good agent who sells property in your price range? ☐

Are they part of the NAEA? ☐

Have you registered your details with several agents? ☐

Have you given them your budget, ideal location and property description? ☐

Have you asked them what's happening in the market at the moment? ☐

The solicitor

Have you chosen a solicitor? ☐

Does he specialise in conveyancing? ☐

Have you asked about his fees and what they include? ☐

Have you got a direct line number so you can speak to him quickly? ☐

Do they use the TransAction scheme? ☐

Have they written confirming your instruction? ☐

Do you have the funds ready to transfer in case of a quick exchange? ☐

The property

Have you found your home yet?

Are you speaking to the agents regularly?

Are you asking all the right questions to save time?

Is the agent on the ball?

Are the viewings a waste of time? If so, change agents.

When viewing are you spotting the potential and not getting sidetracked?

Are you looking for structural danger signs?

Are you taking notes while viewing to prevent any confusion?

Are you asking the sellers some pertinent questions?

Are the neighbours OK?

What local facilities are there?

If it is leasehold, how long is remaining?

What are the service charges, what do they cover and how should they be paid?

Is there a management company or residents' association?

Who is responsible for the outside of the property?

The offer

Are you ready to make an offer?

Are you prepared to negotiate?

Have you told them it is subject to survey and contract? ☐

Have you asked the agent, or joint agents, to take it off the market? ☐

If you are a first-time buyer, or cash buyer, have you told them this? ☐

Have you given all the details to your solicitor and lender? ☐

Are you putting pressure on them for a quick exchange? ☐

Do you have everything you need for your mortgage application? ☐

Have they arranged for a valuation? ☐

As a sign of good intent, would you put down a small deposit? ☐

The survey

Does the property need a survey? ☐

Which kind of survey? ☐

If it is a new house, does it have a NHBC ten-year guarantee? ☐

Have you found a surveyor through personal recommendation? ☐

If not, are you shopping around? ☐

Is he registered ARICS or similar? ☐

How much will it cost? ☐

How quickly can he do the survey? ☐

When you receive the report can you discuss it with him? ☐

Having received the survey and read it, is there anything you need to do? ☐

Do you need a specialist report? ☐

Does the seller need to fix anything? ☐

Can you alter your offer? ☐

The exchange

Are you ready to exchange contracts? ☐

Have you checked the fixtures and fittings list? ☐

Is your solicitor happy with all his investigations? ☐

Is your surveyor happy? ☐

Is your lender happy? ☐

Are you happy? (And not tearing your hair out.) ☐

Is your buildings insurance sorted? ☐

Will the property be empty on completion? ☐

Have you agreed a date for completion? ☐

Is your deposit ready to reach your solicitor prior to exchange? ☐

The completion

Having exchanged, are you ready to complete? ☐

Are you sorting out the move? ☐

Have you booked a van or removal company?

Is the mortgage and any extra money at the ready?

Are you in regular contact with your solicitor?

Is the champagne on ice?

PART TWO

Selling

CHAPTER 5

How to sell

When to sell

The options

The homeseller's pack

Estate agents

Selling privately

When to sell

There really isn't a right or wrong time to sell because presumably circumstances will dictate, more often than not, when you do.

Most agents will tell you that spring is the busiest time of the year, followed by the autumn, and certainly if you want the maximum number of buyers looking around your house, these are ideal times to market it. Obviously the winter months when the trees are bare and your garden, if you have one, is not looking at its best, will not present your home in its most favourable light.

The main thing is not to forget how much time it can take to get your property ready for viewing. In later chapters we shall look at presentation and first impressions, but you really need to be doing this *before* you invite any estate agents round.

So for a spring sale I would recommend starting the process in the second week of January. Here's a possible timetable:

> **January** – create the look (see pages 160–70).
>
> **February** – get three agents round to value the property.
>
> **March** – agent prepares for marketing.
>
> **March/April** – your property goes on the market.

Remember, the agent has a lot to do before he can market your home, such as measuring up to prepare the details, organising the photography and floor plan, preparing the advertising and the printing of the details.

Time spent on the preparatory work can reap considerable benefits when the actual marketing commences.

One good tip, which might help rush the process along a bit, is to have some fabulous photographs taken of your home, on a sunny day with the blossom out against a clear blue sky, whether you are thinking of selling or not. You never know when you might need them. For some obscure reason I had our old house photographed over a year before it went on the market, which proved pretty handy when we came to sell.

Why are you selling?

So why are you selling anyway? Have you thought about the aggro, stress, physical upheaval, emotional turmoil and bad back you're going to get? *There are alternatives you know*, if you don't *have* to move for work or family reasons.

- Build an extension. Up or sideways will give you the extra rooms you need and be cheaper than moving.

- Convert the attic into another bedroom.

- Rent, if your job is relocating, in case you want to come back.

- Let out your home if there is demand in your area and buy another with a Buy to Let mortgage.

- If it's empty nest syndrome, take in B&B guests.

- If it's too big, rent out a wing of the house. (How grand!)

The options

When you sell your home, you have three options as to how quickly you move into your next home.

Option 1

You sell and buy simultaneously. This can be stressful because of the possibility of getting into a chain, but it does cut out any extra costs incurred, such as storage and rent, were you to live somewhere else for the interim period.

Option 2

You sell and rent temporary accommodation while you look around for something suitable to buy, safe in the knowledge that your capital is on deposit and will enable you to move swiftly once your offer has been accepted. This makes you a very attractive buyer. The downside is that while you are looking, prices may be rising alarmingly, thus making your capital appear to shrink. In a rising market, you can't afford to hang around.

Option 3

You exchange contracts on your home but agree an extended period prior to completion, in order to give you time to look for somewhere to buy. This provides excellent breathing space but does depend on the circumstances of your buyer. They will usually *not* be in a chain (thankfully).

Not an option

Whichever option you go for – or find yourself accepting – it is much better than choosing your ideal home and *then* selling your house. Believe me. I've been there. We have even bought the house before selling ours, which is ridiculous. A bridging loan is *not* an attractive prospect and definitely not an option. Well, it is, but you know what I mean. Don't go there.

So, in an ideal world, put your house on the market and get an offer before you start looking.

The Homeseller's Pack

This is designed to speed up the process prior to exchange and is **information supplied by the seller**. Sounds like a good idea but the scheme is still being tested and, until the legislation is passed, is not being adhered to by all solicitors.

However, this is what you, as a seller, should provide:

- a proper surveyor's report;

- the title documents;

- copies of any building regulations, planning permission, consents or listed building regulations;

- copies of any NHBC warranties;

- local authority searches;

- information pertaining to any current problems with the property;

- any guarantees if work has been carried out;

- a draft contract.

And if the property is leasehold:

- a copy of the lease;

- buildings insurance details;

- service charge accounts and amounts payable;

- contact addresses of the freeholder and management company;

- any other strange regulations that may apply.

Estate agents

How to choose the right one for you

I've said this before many times and I'll say it again: 'There *are* some good estate agents out there, but it is up to you to do your homework.'

In all my years of dealing with agents, I have only had one bad experience, and that was because the agent was unutterably dull and lazy. On the whole, they are a bunch of professionals. If they are not, don't use them.

Obviously, if you are selling a modest home in a seaside resort, one of the grander 'country house' agents might start to get a bit snotty, but a small, independent, local agent would be *very* happy to have your business.

TOP TIPS

Here are my eight top tips for selecting the right estate agent.

1. Look at the For Sale boards in your area to see who is selling similar homes to yours.

2. You could check in the local newspapers and magazines as well, to see which agencies are advertising homes like yours.

3. You should pop into a few local agencies to test the waters. Do you get a friendly reception?

4. Some local independent agents have now joined forces with the larger, city-based agencies. This could be useful if you're looking for a country cottage.

5. Do their details look attractive? Is the window display eye-catching? If you get one of those spivvy types or they keep you waiting, walk away.

6. Ask a friend in the area which agent they bought their house from. If their experience was pleasant, that agent might be the one to help you sell.

7. Make sure they are qualified professionals, as most of the problems occur with people who have set themselves up as estate agents without any qualifications at all. It is surprisingly easy to do. They should be ARICS (Associate of the Royal Institute of Chartered Surveyors), or ANAEA (Associate of the National Association of Estate Agents) or ASVA (Associate of the Society of Valuers and Auctioneers). Some are all three!

8. If your home is unusual, or exceptional or historic you may want one of the larger, upmarket agencies who have contacts, or offices, overseas. The national newspapers and glossies will alert you as to who they are.

Once you have decided which agencies you like the look of, choose three to come to your home to give you a valuation. They should have a good look around both inside and out; take their time and not seem hurried, and have good local knowledge of the area.

Make an effort with the presentation of your home, as if the agent was a potential purchaser. He may value your home according to the way it looks and its decorative order. If you are about to paint the bathroom or the exterior of the house, tell him, because this may well make a difference to his valuation.

What it really comes down to in the end is whether you like the agent or not. Do you trust them enough to sell your home? Can you develop a rapport with them? Trust your instincts. If you don't feel comfortable with the person doing the valuation, male or female, then you probably won't want them to sell your home. Not only that, why would you give all that commission to someone you don't even like? If you *do* like them, here are a few questions that you should ask.

QUESTIONS TO ASK... THE ESTATE AGENT

Q What are their fees? These can range from 2 or 3 per cent in the South-East to 1.25 per cent in the North and West. These fees are always open to negotiation and VAT is charged on top. If you have a desirable property in a fabulous location you should be able to do a good deal.

Q What are the agent's qualifications? Make sure he is a professional.

Q Will you be showing the property or will the agent be? Ideally they should do the viewings because you may not be available, don't need the hassle and an agent can sell it for you in a more impartial way.

Q Is the agency open at weekends? Sometimes Saturday staff are students brought in especially, with very little knowledge.

Q Do they charge for advertising in the local paper? How many ads will be appearing?

Q How much will the photographs cost and how many do they use on the details?

Q Will they do a floor plan? If so, how much does it cost?

Q Do they have other offices where your property will be marketed?

Q Do they do mail-outs? If so, how often?

Q Will your details be in the window?

Q Do they insist on sole agency? You may want to go elsewhere as well.

Q Will they put up a For Sale board? You might not want one.

Q Do they have an agency magazine or paper? If so, will your home appear in it?

Q What other marketing do they use?

Q Do they have a website and will your home be on it? Is there an extra charge for this?

Q Ask to see an agreement form and several sets of details, so that you can compare them with other agencies. First impressions are very important and you will find that some details are presented in a much more attractive way.

After you have received your three valuations, sit down and take a deep breath. Chances are that you will be pleasantly surprised at how much your home is worth. However, don't be tempted to go for the highest valuation as this may just be flattery to get your business.

Weigh up the answers to all the questions you have asked and choose the agent who you think will do the best job of selling your home.

Issuing instructions

Call up your chosen agent – always insist on speaking to the same person because this will help to develop the relationship – and tell him that you would like him to sell your home, 'because he was the most professional/the most knowledgeable about the area/the most likely to succeed'. A little flattery goes a long way. Once you have done this – **issued instruction to sell** – the agent should confirm his fees in writing.

You should check carefully how much notice you need to give in case you decide to change agents or how long your agreement with the agent lasts before you can instruct someone else. You don't want to be tied to an agent for 12 weeks if after a month you realise they are useless and you have made a mistake.

UPMARKET AGENCIES

If you own a substantial home and are thinking of approaching one of the upmarket agents, you will have a choice of size and style of the glossy brochure. Be warned that the printing of these is very expensive and some of them use dozens of photographs. In my experience, it is the floor plan that is the most crucial part of any brochure. People are becoming more used to reading floor plans and the photographs are really just the icing on the cake.

Advertising your smart home in the glossy magazines, especially those associated with Scottish castles and baronial halls, is jaw-droppingly expensive. It can run into several thousand pounds for a full-page advertisement and your agent will try to persuade you that it is a necessary part of the marketing. Again, in my experience, the agent is using your money to advertise his agency.

By the time the picture appears in the magazine, most of those homes are already sold. If yours hasn't sold yet it may generate a dozen phone calls, maybe more, but it won't guarantee to sell it. However, you can negotiate all these costs against your commission, which will presumably be a whopping amount.

On a £600,000 house, a 3 per cent commission will come to £18,000 and your extras for advertising and brochures etc. *could* come to as much as £4,500. So don't be shy!

Negotiate on:

- photographs;
- brochures;
- floor plans;
- website;
- newspaper advertising;
- glossy advertising;
- all marketing;
- commission fees.

A lot of these posh agencies have a press office with a PR department having access to all the national publications. Sometimes publicity helps to sell a home, particularly if it is featured in editorial because of its unique/quirky/historic/unusual qualities. Ask them to push the publicity because more people read editorial than adverts. Strange but true.

What is included in the agent's deal?

Once you have chosen your estate agent, communication is vital. Don't just leave them to get on with it because they have dozens of other properties to sell, with all those sellers giving them grief. So **regular contact**, with **humour** and **charm,** will go a long way. Don't hassle them unnecessarily but if you haven't seen the details yet or haven't had a viewing for a few days, give them a call and a gentle nudge. I have found that rather than going on the attack, humour helps.

You must let them know of any timescale involved. For example, you may not want to sell it next week but have put it on the market with a view to selling in a few months' time. Of course this is very tricky to achieve but sometimes a purchaser will agree to exchange contracts with a **delayed completion**. This means they put down their 10 per cent deposit on exchange and will complete when you are ready. However, this is quite unusual, especially if everyone is in a chain.

Your agent should be knowledgeable about the area, enthusiastic, positive, polite and presentable. You should expect the agent to report back after each viewing because getting some feedback does help.

Press him for information about the reaction because it could be that he is holding back on telling you something. Most estate agents are not 'house doctors' and will not advise you on presentation, but if he says there was a 'terrible smell in the kitchen or the hallway was dark', he might be trying to say 'Please empty the bin and replace the light bulbs'. If, however, he is very forthcoming on the state of your home, take his advice, because he knows what sells and what doesn't.

Your agent should be utterly professional. If he starts using bad language, go elsewhere. If he starts getting negative, go elsewhere.

One agent confessed to me that once a property has officially gone on the market, if nothing happens within two weeks, i.e. no offers, they start to get bored with it and move on to the next one. There is a **two-week window** when the agent will have all guns blazing and give it his full energy but after that they will go off the boil. It is up to you, therefore, to keep him focused and working for you. Threaten to go elsewhere if he seems to be flagging.

What to expect from the estate agent

- Every time there is to be a viewing, your agent should ring to inform you, even if they are holding keys, because you may be at home that day.

- The agent should get to the property before the client – especially if you are *not* there – to open up and turn on the lights or whatever is necessary.

- If you are at home make yourself scarce because some would-be purchasers are intimidated by the owner being present. The agent can be impartial. If they return for a second viewing, however, this is usually good news and it can be helpful if you are around then to answer questions.

- The agent should be talking all through the viewing, about the efficient central heating and the wonderful parks etc.! If he stands silently by the front door, fire him.

- You must like your agent and develop a rapport with him. It is important that you feel he is honest and trustworthy.

The commission and costs

We have already seen that the commission to your agent is a considerable sum of money. If your home sold for, say, £100,000, at 2 per cent commission that is £2,000 (plus VAT) you are giving away. As we have already established, you can negotiate this fee, but beware of any **extra costs**. You may be charged for the advertising, the marketing or for being on their website.

Some agencies don't charge for any of these services but it is best to ask first because they can be expensive, depending on the size of your property.

Sole agency or multi-agency?

If you only issue instruction to one agency to sell your house this is called **sole agency** and your commission fee will be negotiated accordingly. If you decide to place it with several agents in order to spread the marketing and hopefully ensnare a buyer more quickly, the fee will usually be half a per cent higher. They are working in competition with each other but the fee will only go to whoever introduces the buyer. This is called multi-agency.

If you decide to put your home on the market with two agents who will work together on the marketing, and split the commission, this is called **joint sole agency** (JSA). The fee for JSA is also half a per cent higher than sole agency.

> For example, a London agent could charge:
> Sole agency – 2.5% + VAT (elsewhere it can be 1.75%)
> Multi-agency – 3% + VAT
> JSA   – 3% + VAT

Most properties only need to be with one agent, unless you don't mind spending the extra money. There is a certain amount of cross-fertilisation among agencies anyway.

> Try to avoid something called **'sole selling rights'** with your agent, because if you happen to sell the house yourself to a friend or relative, some agencies will insist on their commission. They should only take commission if the buyer was introduced by them.

When to change agencies

It is such an emotionally charged and stressful time, when you are selling your home, that it is hardly surprising that most agents get it in the neck if nothing happens for a while.

Before you have agreed terms and signed the conditions, make absolutely sure you are not locked into an exclusive arrangement for months on end. Read the small print, because you may find that if you are unhappy with your agent, you are unable to move for a specified time.

Most agents insist on six weeks after it has officially gone on the market and I think that's fair. Give them a chance, for heaven's sake! Advertising lead-times (the time between placing the ad and publication) mean that sometimes your home won't appear in the publication for three weeks.

If, after that time, you get very few viewings or feel that you are not getting the right attention, it is time to move on. Shop around again and choose another suitable agent. You may already have a second choice but ask the first agent why he feels your home is 'sticking'. It could be something you could so easily rectify or it could be overpriced.

Saturation point

The time to change agents is when they have marketed your home and arranged several viewings but for some reason you haven't received any offers. Sometimes many weeks can go by without a viewing and the property will be seen to be 'sticking'. Unfortunately, your agent will have reached saturation point and will be far more interested in the newer properties he is currently dealing with. This is the time to put your home with a new agent who has a fresh approach.

If your home is not selling, there might be something wrong

with it! Sorry to be so blunt but it's true. It may be overpriced or lacking the appropriate presentation. Take a long, hard look at your home (see Chapter 6 on Presentation) or ask a friend for their honest opinion. It may not be only the agent you need to change!

Small independent or large High Street names?

I have dealt with large and small agencies over the years, and they both have benefits and drawbacks, but it really comes down to what sort of property you are selling, the price you would like to achieve and whether you want to be a small fish in a big pond or vice versa.

I suppose I have always been of the opinion that small is beautiful. Small is certainly more personal when it comes to estate agents. You don't get swallowed up in the machinery of a large company.

For example, a small local agent will know the area well, whereas one of the larger chains will have staff from all over the place.

Don't be impressed by the familiar High Street names, as the smaller agents, who may only have one office, have a higher incentive to sell your home. One agent with a small agency told me, 'We are not governed by a large corporation and do not offer financial services but we do provide a very personal service with expert local knowledge'.

You will find with the smaller agencies that they specialise in one specific area of the market and it's not necessarily the lower end. One top agent I dealt with many years ago was specialising in houses at the upper end of the bracket, but he only had one office. He was competing with the big companies but his service and style were unique and his brochures were fabulous. He now has two offices!

Some small agencies share the commission among the whole company rather than have their negotiators competing with each other. This makes for a less pushy, aggressive style. Also, you tend to only deal with one person in the office, which I happen to like because you can get to know them and use emotional pressure, if necessary. In the large agencies there are so many people all running around like headless chickens that you never deal with the same person twice. When you want to speak to them they are 'out of the office' because they spend the whole time on viewings.

Of course, the advantages of putting your home with a large company, whether it is formal or not, are that they have a built-in network of offices and offer a marketing service that is often global. Most of them now have offices overseas, so if you are selling the sort of property that might interest a Japanese businessman, this sort of international company is the one for you.

You are less likely to get the naughty tricks from the older, established agencies but they still employ young men, with a strong competitive edge. This is where the aggressive sales talk comes in. Don't be taken in by it and try to put yourself in the shoes of the buyer. If you think your buyer might find the patter nauseating too, don't use that agent.

It all comes down to your personality and instincts. A small, smart agency is going to do just as good a job as the bigger High Street ones. Remember, the smaller ones are hungrier!

Floor plans, details and photos

As I've said before, when buying a property the floor plan can be a terrific help, therefore it goes without saying that if you are *selling* a property, *insist* on a floor plan. It doesn't matter whether it is a two-bedroom flat or a vast Georgian mansion, the floor plan will be invaluable.

Small agency?

For:

- personal service;
- specialises in local area;
- higher incentive to sell;
- you deal with one person.

Against:

- may not get the plum properties;
- no network of offices;
- may not have a website;
- no international marketing.

Large agency?

For:

- network of offices;
- international marketing;
- upmarket image;
- has a website;
- plenty of staff.

Against:

- may lack personal service;
- will be more expensive;
- may put off some buyers;
- the rapid turnover of properties means they get bored with yours more quickly;
- it can take ages to get your property on the market.

The buyer will see your details and immediately be able to make sense of the layout of your home. This is why floor plans are so wonderful. (See Chapter 3 for more on details and floor plans.)

The photos are another story. The camera can deceive and tell downright lies with its magic lens. It can obscure and obliterate the bad bits (you don't see the main road in the photograph) and enhance the good bits (it can make the garden look huge), so that your humble abode looks like Buckingham Palace. (That's assuming you've got a whiz photographer.)

Discuss beforehand which aspect is most likely to sell your home (it doesn't have to be the front of the building, if you have a wonderful kitchen or amazing back garden) and insist on seeing the results before they run off 250 copies for their details. They may decide to use more than one photo, in which case make sure you are there on the day and that everything looks perfect.

TOP TIPS

Here are my five top tips on photographing the exterior of your home.

1. The exterior should only be photographed on a bright, sunny day.

2. The front door must be immaculate. Repaint it if necessary.

3. Put some flowers or shrubs on either side of the front door.

4. The garden should look fabulous with newly mown grass.

5. Take down net curtains and clean the windows.

TOP TIPS

Here are my five top tips on photographing the interior of your home.

1. Tidy up the room that is being photographed.

2. If there is a fireplace, light the fire. (It doesn't matter what time of year it is.)

3. Adjust the furniture slightly to create the most pleasing angles. The room must *not* look cluttered.

4. Switch on table lamps and use flowers to lighten, or fill, a corner.

5. Make sure any interesting features are shown clearly in the photographs – such as original flooring; plaster cornicing; bay windows etc.

> If the property is empty the photographer should concentrate on the exterior only. However, if there are some beautiful features such as fireplaces, cornicing or balustrading, use arty close-ups on the details. Developers often go to the expense of hiring furniture to make the photo look good. There's nothing worse than an expanse of beige carpet.

Selling privately – doing it yourself

This is not for the faint-hearted. If you really do begrudge an estate agent his commission fee then you can set about selling your home yourself. It will make the whole process even *more* stressful and, of course, there is expense involved in the marketing of your home. You will have to think about:

- preparing and producing the details;
- fixing a price;

- printing the details;

- taking photographs;

- measuring the rooms;

- placing advertisements in newspapers, magazines and on the internet;

- answering the phone;

- arranging viewings.

One lady who tried this said that about half the people who arranged to view her house didn't turn up and, as a busy young executive, she knew that time is money.

The internet has made selling privately much easier, and there are several sites dedicated to putting buyers and sellers in direct contact with each other, but it is all very time-consuming.

> I've said this before but your personal security is of paramount importance, so it is worth repeating. If you are a single female selling your home this way, you *must* have a friend with you when you are showing viewers around. Preferably a male friend.

If you want to sell your home privately, all the newspapers and magazines have a property section where you can place an advertisement. The weekend national newspapers are probably the best for this. The glossies do it too but they have a very long lead-time and are *very* expensive.

Make your ad as eye-catching as possible (it might be worth putting it in a box so that it stands out a bit), because usually there are no photographs, only words. Remember to include:

- the number of bedrooms;

- whether it is freehold or leasehold;

- the location;

- the age of the building;

- number of reception rooms;

- any special or quirky features;

- the size of the garden;

- the price;

- your phone number.

It could read something like:

'Unique chapel conversion dating back to 1825 in a quiet Somerset village. 3 bedrooms, 2 bathrooms, 3 receptions, mezzanine floor. Freehold. £225,000. Phone Duncan on blah blah blah for details.'

Alternatively:
'Recently converted loft space. Ultra-modern décor and fittings. 2,500 sq ft. Docklands. Must see. 350,000K o.n.o. Call Jules on...'

Get the picture? Short and snappy is good but you must hook them with one or two words. **Unique** and **ultra-modern** in these examples. When people start calling they will want you to send details with a picture so have these ready to mail out. The downside to all this is that you will inevitably get some time-wasters who just want to look around. You have no way of knowing whether they are serious buyers or if they have the means to buy.

If someone makes an offer, it is up to you to negotiate and it depends how brave or tough you are. You have no intermediary to act for you to ascertain how high the buyer will go. Sometimes an agent has information that he can pass on to the vendor such as 'I know he'll go to 260K but that's his absolute final offer'. If you don't know this you may accept his offer of 240K, thinking he won't go any higher.

Anyway, good luck. All I know is that it is quite a delicate matter getting the price you want but not losing the buyer in the process. You could always ask your solicitor to do the negotiating, I suppose. As soon as the sale price is agreed get the purchaser's solicitor in touch with your solicitor, so that the contracts can be drawn up.

However, it may be wise to keep on showing your home until exchange of contracts as there is many a slip between the ship and the wharf, and I have heard of people pulling out of a deal, even after surveys etc., on the day they were due to exchange.

CHECKLIST

Selling it yourself checklist

Prepare some details with photographs. ☐

Write an eye-catching advertisement. ☐

Place ad in newspapers or on the internet. ☐

Arrange viewings every half-hour to suit you. ☐

Send out details. ☐

Have a friend with you during viewings. ☐

Be tough but not greedy when you negotiate. ☐

Accept a good offer. ☐

Instruct a solicitor. The conveyancing fees will be the same, even though you've sold it yourself. ☐

Keep showing until you exchange contracts. ☐

CHAPTER 6

Achieving your market potential

First impressions outside

First impressions inside

I cannot stress strongly enough how crucial the first impression of your home will be to prospective buyers. They will make a judgement within the first few seconds, so the way you present the outside of your house or flat could make or break a sale. Once they are inside there are further stumbling blocks, but first you must draw them inside with an appealing, positive view.

First impressions outside – kerb appeal

Even if you share a house that has been converted into many flats, it is worth taking into account what the buyer may think before entering your flat. Overflowing dustbins and an abandoned bicycle in the front garden do not send out the right message.

So here are a few tips to help you present the exterior of your home to its maximum advantage. This is now known as **kerb appeal**.

- Make sure the approach to the front door is clear of any obstacles. Remove bicycles, prams, toys, buggies, rollerblades etc. from the path and porch.

- The name or number of the house should be clearly visible. There is nothing more annoying than not being able to find the property.

- If there is a garden gate it should be clean and freshly painted and left open to welcome people towards the house. A closed gate seems negative.

- Make sure the front garden is neat and tidy. Clip the hedges, mow the lawn, weed flower beds and trim roses or brambles. Even the tiniest space can look shambolic, so tidy it all up.

- Dustbins are a real eyesore. If your house is divided into flats and all your bins are at the front you can hide them away with a length of fencing or bamboo sheeting attached to a timber frame. If it is an improvement, the other residents could hardly object.

- The front door should look glossy and fresh. (Blue seems to be the most successful door colour for selling houses!) Polish up the brass letterbox and knocker.

- If the window frames need repainting I'm afraid you should repaint them. If it is shabby and peeling outside, the viewer will assume it is shabby and peeling inside and may not come in.

- Remove hoses and tools.

- You could add colour to the front with seasonal flowers in some tubs or window-boxes. This can make all the difference and, when you've sold, you can take the whole lot with you!

- Sparkling clean windows are a must.

- A neat trick is to replace the light bulb in the porch with a higher wattage for those winter evenings.

- Remember you must do all these things *before* viewings commence. You don't want people tripping over paint pots and ladders.

DRIVE-BYS

These are the scourge of the home seller and are rapidly developing into a new trend. This is when the buyer receives details of your property, then drives by to take a look at the exterior before making an appointment to view. This can be very depressing if the interior is more fabulous than the exterior, because the potential buyer may not even wish to view based on what he has seen.

Don't forget the garden

If you have a garden, however small, it is a major selling point as people attach enormous importance to having some outside space. Therefore, spend a little time making sure it looks its best.

I'm not suggesting that you get in the landscape designers and remodel your garden entirely, although that would probably look wonderful, but to think about how best to present your garden. It will certainly add to the appeal of your property if there is a nice aspect across the garden from your sitting-room. If it is neat and tidy it will make it much more sellable.

If you have children and the garden has become one enormous playground covered in bald patches, please don't leave it like that. A small investment in some new turf, a few shrubs, a repaired fence and a tidy-up could add thousands to the price. Honestly.

If you are a keen gardener and have lovingly tended your garden for years, the estate agent should draw attention to this in the details as it is a major selling point. I know of one lady who bought a house based on the beauty of the garden alone, without even stepping inside the house!

Garden ideas

- If you buy a brand new home, planting out mature trees and hedging will instantly add value to your house as it will set it apart from the rest. But remember, first-time buyers like gardens that are easy to maintain.

- If you are buying a flat, then a garden will obviously add value to the property. Garden flats are immensely popular, particularly if you have spent an extra bit on security. Use the garden as an extra room to add value to the property. For example, in summer it could become the dining room.

- If you live in a city, a garden is not an expectation but a bonus. If you have 25 ft you are considered lucky. Make the most of it.

- If you have a roof garden then make it as lavish and well stocked as possible. You will add value only by making it look like an oasis of calm and not like an old roof with a couple of discarded Christmas trees on it!

- A garden with a wonderful view will definitely add to the value.

- The way people view the landscape is an integral part of buying a home.

First impressions inside – presentation

Now that you have given your property a facelift on the outside, you need to consider the inside. The presentation of your property from the moment a person steps through your door is going to make the difference between receiving an offer quickly and having your property 'stick' on the market. The biggest problem we all have is **clutter**. We all have it, collect it and keep it. Heaven knows why. We need to get rid of all the clutter in order to present a tidy, spacious, calm environment that someone would really like to buy. So, chuck out everything and be ruthless. Family photos, especially, can be very distracting so put them all away.

The hallway

Because this is the first space that your buyers will see it is important that you do the following to prevent them making a snap decision.

- Wash down walls and doors that may be splattered with rain and mud; or if it is any colour other than neutral, I'm afraid it will have to be painted. I'm sorry but it won't take long. One-coat paint is available in soft creams and neutrals, which will make the hallway much lighter and more appealing.

- Put away all coats, hats, dog leads, etc.

- Replace light bulbs (with higher wattage, if necessary).

- Clean hall mats or rugs.

- Remove racks of boots and shoes.

- Hang a large mirror to increase light.

- Flowers are always a lovely bonus but not essential, as this can get expensive.

- If there are lots of pictures, take them down. One or two will do.

The rest of the house

The same rules apply.

- Keep all the rooms well aired, as there is nothing worse than a house that smells musty or damp.

- Complete any little unfinished DIY jobs. If the bathroom is half-tiled and you can't be bothered to finish it, get someone in to do it for you. It will be money well spent.

- Tidy, tidy and tidy again.

- The route around the property should be free of obstruction, i.e. don't walk into the sitting room and into the back of a chair. Move it and open up the space.

- Don't hide things behind a door. All doors must open fully.

- De-clutter the kitchen completely and clean it like mad. It must sparkle. Chuck out anything that doesn't have a useful role.

- Remove any unnecessary furniture. Space is what people want.

- Take down any old curtains that may look a bit past it. No curtains at all is better than bad curtains. Let them see the windows.

- Estate agents say that most viewers walk into a room and make a beeline for the window, so keep the route clear.

- The bathroom must be clutter-free and really, *really* clean. Throw away empty shampoo bottles, and if you have a shower curtain that has seen better days, buy a new one.

- Leave the loo seat down. Always!

- The sitting room must have a focal point. Ideally it would be a fireplace but, if you don't have one, a piece of furniture will do with a picture or mirror above it.

- If your sofa is looking tired, use a throw to cover it and add a couple of nice cushions.

- Make sure all the windows are clean.

- Make all the beds. Nicely.

Give yourself an extra ten minutes every morning to tidy up before leaving for work, in case there is a viewing in your absence. (See checklist on page 176).

Kitchens and bathrooms – the secret code

The two most important rooms, which influence the sale of your home, are the **kitchen and bathroom**. Women, particularly, are swayed by these rooms more than any other, so it would be wise to fix them up first if you want a quick sale.

If you have already followed my advice about space, light and presentation but feel there is still something lacking, it could be that some drastic measures are required.

GETTING OUT THE PAINT POT

Paint is the most wonderful product for effecting a rapid, in-expensive transformation, so get those brushes out. I absolutely love painting and often do the refurbishment of my rental flats myself. I find it very therapeutic, but if you feel unsure get some help. A friend might help, or the local handyman or decorator. (These can be found in your local newspaper or ask at the post office.) Remember, if you want to leave your house the way it is, then fine. That's your decision. However, with a little motivation, it could give your home the edge and increase the asking price.

Obviously, if you are just about to leave a place, you might not feel inclined to start spending money on it, but believe me, even on a very tight budget you can achieve amazing results.

When I'm doing the painting myself, I use **paint pads** to apply emulsion to the walls. Decorators sniff at these but I think they are quick and easy to use and you only need apply one coat. I can do a whole room in half a day! They are available at all DIY stores.

The kitchen quick fix

Transforming your kitchen need not be expensive and could add thousands to the asking price. You may need to do some or all of the following.

- Use an abrasive cleaner to really clean the kitchen and to remove all the grease. Most of the paintwork will immediately look better and you can see what needs doing.

- If they need it, paint the walls in white emulsion and the doors and windows in white eggshell.

- Take down curtains/blinds/pelmets.

- If the cupboard fronts are very old-fashioned you can replace them with new doors (keep them plain and neutral) or paint them white.

- If the vinyl flooring is dark or old-fashioned, replace it with a light-coloured vinyl. Most carpet warehouses do offcuts.

- If you're feeling brave you could lay wood laminate flooring instead. It instantly makes a room look more glamorous.

- If there is a tiled splashback that is dark or old-fashioned (anything patterned or coloured), you could tile over it with cheap white tiles from the DIY store, or even paint over them.

If you follow the list above the results will be amazing. But, most important, *do not* replace any of the clutter! Just some white china, olive oil bottles and a fruit bowl will do. Remember, you are selling a lifestyle as well. You will have to live in a very purist, tidy way until you have sold I'm afraid.

These are just suggestions and ideas. Obviously if you have a wonderful country-style kitchen with an Aga and timber beams then a fresh lick of paint to walls and woodwork will probably do. But keep it tidy.

Bathroom

I'm afraid that white is the only colour that a bathroom suite should be. If yours is not white, never mind. I'm not going to suggest that you change it, but there are some things you need to do.

- Scrub the bathroom free of grime until it sparkles.

- Paint the walls a soft white vinyl silk.

- Replace any broken tiles and paint over the ones with dodgy patterns (use masking tape and a primer).

- If the tiles are already white, regrout where it has gone brown.

- Install a huge, frameless mirror.

- Replace shower curtain or scrub shower glass.

- Replace fluffy coloured bath mats with plain white cotton mats instead.

- Replace carpet (if you have it) with vinyl floor covering in the palest cream or ceramic floor tiles.

- Install a wooden loo seat if you haven't already got one.

- Use brighter light bulbs.

- Buy some new white towels. (You can take these with you.)

- Reseal around the bath.

- Toilet should be sparkling clean, smell nice and have loo seat down.

- If the whole family use this bathroom, keep the children's toys out of sight. It has to look like a grown-ups' bathroom.

Space and light

These are the two words that estate agents use the most often with regard to a viewing. Giving the illusion of having both are crucial if you are to succeed in achieving your market potential.

Some people live in homes where light is in short supply and space is something to dream about. There are several things you can do to give the illusion of space and light.

CHECKLIST

Creating light and space checklist

Take down curtains to let in the light. If you have a lovely bay window, why hide it? ☐

Take down roller blinds if they are not necessary. The kitchen doesn't need blinds (unless you like cooking in the buff!). ☐

Install little spotlights in the kitchen to light every corner. ☐

Use uplighters in the sitting room to bounce light off the ceiling. ☐

Replace any broken light bulbs. ☐

Use a higher wattage in the hallway. ☐

Remove some pieces of furniture if they are getting in the way of viewing. Less is more. ☐

Corridors and doorways must be unobstructed. A laundry basket behind the bathroom door, for example, is not a good idea. ☐

Tidy up and de-clutter as I mentioned before. *Space* is the key word here. If necessary you can box everything up in readiness for your move. ☐

If you are fond of strong colours on the walls this will not be creating light. A burgundy sitting room or royal blue bedroom is fine while you are living there, but not for selling. Neutral colours will appeal to a broader market, so invest in some paint – white or cream – and get painting.

Clean all the windows and keep remaining curtains well drawn back.

TOP TIPS

Here are my five top tips for achieving a quick sale.

1. If you want a quick sale make sure that you have your deeds ready or that you know where they are. They are either with the lender or maybe your solicitor. If you can't find them you will have to apply to the Land Registry for a copy, which takes time.

2. Make sure your solicitor knows all about your service charge – if you have one – and whether there are any impending works. This will save time.

3. If you are not good at such things, get someone to help you fix all those annoying broken bits that didn't get fixed. When viewing a property the purchaser will always notice the things that haven't been fixed rather than the things that have.

4. Remember the lifestyle trick. Smart books lying around or a designer suit on the back of the door will impress the buyer.

5. Finally, keep it simple. The buyer wants to be able to envisage himself living there. If you *depersonalise* your home this will be much easier.

CHAPTER 7

Putting your home on view

Attracting the buyer

What to do if your home isn't selling

Selling in Scotland

There are several ways to attract a potential buyer to your property. Bearing in mind that there may well be stiff competition in the market, you have got to present your home effectively and efficiently in order to achieve a sale.

Firstly, your chosen estate agent must market your property correctly.

Secondly, your house must be absolutely ready for viewings.

Thirdly, the agent must know the way to show your house to maximum effect.

Fourthly, there must be as many viewings as possible.

Attracting the buyer

How to handle the viewings

Most estate agents will agree that a viewing will go more smoothly if there are no children present, especially if there is a baby in the house. However, if you want to be present during the viewings, perhaps you could make arrangements for someone to look after the little darlings for a while. A screaming baby is not conducive to creating an illusion of calm.

Similarly, pets can be a hazard if your buyer is not an animal lover. It might make him rush through the viewing, missing all the finer details. Bear this in mind and keep them out of the way.

Showing it yourself

If you have agreed to show the property yourself instead of letting the agent do all the work, there is a certain amount of skill and diplomacy required. The tendency is usually to 'oversell' the property, blinding the viewer with too much information. It is imperative that you *do not do this*. It is important to remember the finer features of your home and any local information that you feel may be of interest to the buyer. Don't be tempted to keep talking to fill in those awkward silences, because the viewer needs to be left alone to imagine what it must be like to live there.

Start with the living room and then follow the general order of your rooms as per your sale particulars, slowly making your way upstairs. If the viewer does not have a copy of the details, it would be useful to hand a copy to them with a pen, in order that they can make notes.

After they have seen everything inside (try to avoid stating the obvious by saying things like 'and this is the bathroom'), take them outside and show them the garden and any outbuildings you may have. Again, try not to say too much. Let them use their imagination. If planning permission has been recently granted for anything such as an extension or a garage, let them know because this is crucially important.

When you have finished showing them around ask them if they would like a cup of tea, or if they have any questions for you. This is their opportunity to ask you about the locale, the neighbours, the parking, the shops, etc. They will also want to know about council tax, water rates, service charges (if any), ground rent, the residents' association and so on, so make sure you have all this information at your fingertips.

> Some viewers would rather view the property unaccompanied. If that is the case it is up to you to make a personal assessment of the situation. Obviously you don't want the family silver going missing, so make sure you see them off the premises.

Giving keys to the agent

In my experience it is far wiser, and less hassle, to let the estate agent handle all the viewings. They have all the professional patter and are more experienced at showing people around a property. If you are employed or working strange hours it is much simpler to give the keys to your agent, so that viewings can be arranged in your absence during normal working hours. Obviously, if a viewing is requested after office hours, the agent may well ask you to do the viewing, but these are rare. Most estate agents have a strict key-handling policy and are scrupulous about security, but always ask what their policy is on giving out keys.

> If you discover that lights have been left on, doors left ajar or, even worse, the bed looks as if it has been used, complain immediately. If the agent tries to pass the buck or gives you lame excuses, you could report them to the NAEA (The National Association of Estate Agents) (see Useful Addresses), which has a strict code of practice.

Having a viewing open day

This practice is commonplace in the United States where 'open days' are usually held on Sundays and anyone can view a property without an appointment. I used to think this was great fun when I was living in Los Angeles, because you can turn up unannounced at some pink marble mansion, have a good gawp and get coffee and cookies thrown in to boot.

This is now catching on here in the UK where an estate agent will advertise an open day for a certain property, particularly a very popular one where viewings are in high demand. This helps to save the estate agent's time and allows you to view the property at your own pace. 'Open days' are usually advertised in the local papers or you will be notified by the agent on receiving the particulars of the property.

Why are you selling?

How you answer this question, when asked by a prospective purchaser, is absolutely crucial if you are to make a sale. Sometimes honesty is *not* the best policy. For example, 'We hate the area, we can't ever park outside the house' is unlikely to persuade them to buy. Similarly, 'The traffic noise has finally become too much'. It would be far better to say something vague such as 'My husband is being relocated' or 'We're moving to the country'.

Don't say:

- the house is too small;

- we hate the neighbours;

- the location was never right.

Do say:

- we've always loved living here and are really unhappy to be moving;

- we love the area;

- you'll be very happy here.

CHECKLIST

Viewing checklist

Here are a few things that you must remember to do before you go to work each day, if the agent is showing your property in your absence.

Make the bed and tidy the bedroom. ☐

Tidy up the bathroom and put the loo seat down. ☐

Open all curtains. ☐

Do washing up and tidy kitchen. ☐

Take out any smelly rubbish, throw away dead flowers, change cat litter tray if any. A pleasant smell when entering the house is imperative. Use one of those smelly plug-ins if necessary. ☐

Check all light bulbs are working and leave on a light if you feel it is necessary. ☐

Make sure all corridors are clear of clutter. ☐

Make sure the hallway, front door, porch area and the approach to the front door are clean and tidy. ☐

If you live in a flat it may be worth warning your neighbours that viewings are taking place, so that they know not to park their bicycle in the hall. ☐

Obviously, it goes without saying that your home should be spotlessly clean during viewings. If housework brings you out in a rash, there will be several cleaning agencies listed in the *Yellow Pages* or in your local paper who can work miracles in a couple of hours. I would highly recommend using a professional cleaner because they can see things that homeowners seem to ignore.

What to do if your home isn't selling

There is nothing worse than having your property 'sticking' on the market. Estate agents are notorious for getting bored with a property after a few weeks, so if you haven't received any offers after several viewings, it may be worth discussing this with your agent. They are bound to say that 'things are very quiet at the moment', but don't allow them to brush you off if you feel that your house is overpriced.

Being greedy and holding out for an **unrealistic price** will only delay your sale, so it may be worth consulting other agents to ask their opinion. Checking house prices in the local paper or in other agent's windows should give you a clearer idea of whether to lower the price or not. It is up to you to make that decision, but always listen to your agent's advice.

Alternatively, it might not be the price at all. It could be that you are **not presenting your home** in the most appealing way to achieve its market potential. Take a long, hard look around or ask a friend to be brutally honest. You might not like what you hear, but it could make all the difference. (See page 163 on First Impressions).

Selling in Scotland

Much of the detail regarding selling in Scotland has already been covered in Chapter 4 in the section on Buying in Scotland, as the procedure is basically the same. The main difference to selling in England is that your solicitor can act as your estate agent as well, so you would be wise to alert your solicitor to the fact that you are about to sell your home before putting it on the market. This is because the process is so speedy in Scotland, compared to

England, with the sale being concluded very quickly after the formal offer has been accepted. Your solicitor will need to:

- make sure your title deeds are in order;

- check the amount remaining on any loan;

- make local authority searches.

Your solicitor can then advertise and arrange for viewings of your home, deal with any offers and then transfer the title deeds to the buyer after repaying your loan. If you are not selling through a solicitor you can go through the normal channels of selling through an estate agent, or even sell the house yourself. When an offer has been received and accepted and the 'missives' have been concluded your solicitor will send the title deeds of the property to the buyer's solicitor, so that he can prepare the disposition.

CHAPTER 8

The offer

Accepting the offer – is the price right?

Renegotiating

Exchange of contracts

Completing the procedure

Final checklist for selling your home

CASE STUDY

Back in 1989 a friend of mine put her house on the market for £160,000. Four weeks later she was offered £149,000 with the promise of a rapid exchange, but turned the offer down. The buyer would not increase his offer and went away. Several weeks went by and we all know what happened at the end of 1989! The market crashed and my friend had to lower the price of her house to £150,000. A week later she was offered £135,000 and procrastinated for two whole days, by which time her second buyer had put in an offer elsewhere.

My friend was now in such a state that she was hitting the bottle big time and her roots needed doing. Another buyer came along and offered her £130,000, but was stuck in a chain and couldn't give her a date for exchange of contracts. She decided to accept this offer and was prepared to wait. She was now faintly hysterical. As Christmas neared and the market continued to plummet, her buyer changed his offer to £125,000. She felt powerless to argue and accepted with a developing sense of doom. To cut a very long story short, the sale went through, eventually, at £125,000, which was a cool £24,000 less than her initial offer.

The moral of this story is that had she accepted the first offer and not been greedy she would have saved herself a lot of money and aggravation.

Accepting the offer

There are several elements that come into play when accepting an offer. For example, if your buyer needs no mortgage, has nowhere to sell and offers you well below the asking price, he knows that he is in a very strong bargaining position. You must now decide whether you can negotiate a higher price than his offer. This is often a tactic deployed by buyers in a strong position. You relent a little on the price, he comes up a little on his offer, you come down a little bit more, he comes up further and eventually you meet in the middle. You as the seller must weigh up the pros and cons, because you could find yourself waiting ages for a similar offer, which is accompanied by all the usual complications, such as timescale and being in a chain.

Your estate agent will do the negotiating for you, based on your instruction. However, there have been occasions in the past when I have been buying property and have found myself being pushed up price-wise by the agent. If I feel my offer is fair, I will warn him that it is 'my full and final offer' and he must go back to the seller to tell him that. Basically, I am saying 'No more games. This is it.

Negotiating is never easy and it is only after years of experience that I have learned to read the signs.

Don't allow yourself to be hassled if you need time to think about an offer. Sleep on it and make a decision the following day. *Do not procrastinate.*

Your house	£120,000
Mr A offers (no complications cash buyer)	£105,000
Mr B offers (has to wait to sell his house)	£110,000

Which offer should you accept? Well, in my opinion you would be safer accepting Mr A's offer. You could exchange and complete in the time it takes for Mr B to even get a sniff.

However, it is hard for me to generalise in a situation like this, because every house sale is different and you should seek advice from your agent and solicitor. Some properties are so desirable that the price keeps going up and eventually you find your home going to **sealed bids** (see page 98) with the final price £60,000 more than you were asking for! This is a wonderful situation to find yourself in and it does happen, but it usually means that the property was undervalued in the first place.

Renegotiating

There is a possibility that after your buyer has received his surveyor's report, he will want to renegotiate the price, because of what has been revealed. This is fairly common practice if the survey has thrown up something really serious, such as subsidence requiring underpinning or a severely damaged roof. Your solicitor will advise you on lowering the agreed sale price because the buyer will sometimes want to take advantage of the situation. You may want to seek professional advice on how much the restoration will cost in order to adjust your price accordingly.

I have known situations in the past where the buyer will suddenly drop his offer by £15,000, because the survey has suggested that one small section of guttering needs replacing. Well, I am sorry, that doesn't cost £15,000, so you might want to consider undertaking the works yourself prior to exchange of contract, so that there can be no argument.

> Be realistic. You don't want to lose your sale by being stubborn.

Gazumping

As a buyer there is nothing more horrible than discovering that you have been gazumped. This is when your offer has been accepted on the home of your dreams and you have started the legal procedures, only to discover that the seller has accepted a higher offer, or is threatening to sell it to somebody else, unless you increase your offer.

So, now that you are selling a property do you really want to employ such dirty tricks? If you have ever been a **gazumpee** you will never be a **gazumper**, because you know how awful it is. However, there is a little red devil in all of us, who is easily tempted by some extra cash. If you find yourself in a situation where somebody is offering you more money for your property, after you have already accepted an offer, it is entirely between you and your conscience. Discuss it with your agent. If he's in the 'dodgy category' he might well say 'let's take it', but in my experience my agents have always said it's either too late to accept another offer, or they suggest going to sealed bids.

Your buyer may insist on a pre-contract deposit agreement, which is designed to prevent gazumping. Each side pays a deposit of 1.5 per cent of the purchase price to a stakeholder and signs an agreement that they will exchange contracts within four weeks. If one side reneges on the deal both deposits go to the other side.

Breaking the chain

Having already addressed the problems of being in a chain in Chapter 4 of this book, you will appreciate that when selling and buying simultaneously, the risk is increased several fold. Unless the person who is buying your home is a first-time buyer or a cash buyer, you will inevitably find yourself in a chain. This, of course, can affect the home that you are hoping to buy and can make the whole process extremely stressful, if your buyer decides to pull out at the last minute.

Some agents now participate in a chain-linking scheme, whereby they will arrange to buy your house at a slightly lower price, based on a proper valuation, so that your sale can go ahead without breaking the chain. The agent will then sell the house in order to recoup his costs, but if he is able to sell for more than the agreed valuation the difference will go to the seller.

Lock-outs

If you have accepted an offer from a buyer he or she may well insist on a lock-out agreement. This is to prevent you continuing to show the property to others with the possibility of accepting a higher offer. Sometimes it can be a purely verbal arrangement and on other occasions money will exchange hands. You the seller give the buyer the exclusive right to buy your house in return for a fee on condition that contracts are exchanged within a specific time. This agreement should be drawn up by your solicitor.

Contract races

If several offers have been made on your house for exactly the same amount, it is possible for your solicitor to advise the buyer's solicitors that they are now in a contract race. He will send out contracts to each of them and the first one to return it, signed, will get your house. This can be a wonderful way to speed up the process to exchange of contracts, but I have known situations where all the buyers pulled out simultaneously, each fearing that they would lose the property.

Exchange of contracts

Hurrah, Hurrah! Assuming that your buyer is happy with the survey, all the searches have been completed and both solicitors have completed all procedures, you are now in a position to exchange contracts. For such a momentous occasion it can be a remarkable anti-climax, because there is no official signing session with a quill and hot wax! Your solicitor will simply ring you, to tell you that you have exchanged. The buyer will have deposited 10 per cent of the asking price in your solicitor's holding account and a date for completion will have been agreed between you and your buyer.

This could be anything from two days to six months later.

Completing the procedure

While you start planning the move, clearing out the attic and arranging everything for your new home, your solicitor will be finalising all the paperwork in readiness for completion. On the agreed date, with both contracts signed, the money will be transferred into your bank account and as soon as the money has arrived, your buyer will technically be the new owner of your home. All keys, including the spare sets, should be left with your agent to hand over to the owner. All that is left for you to do is clear off!

FINAL CHECKLIST FOR SELLING YOUR HOME

Step-by-step checklist for selling your home

Before putting it on the market

Are you sure you really want to sell? ☐

Have you decided when to sell? ☐

Are you going to sell and buy simultaneously or sell and rent temporarily? ☐

Have you notified your solicitor that you are selling? ☐

Have you prepared the Homeseller's Pack? ☐

Have you asked three agents to value your property? ☐

Have you chosen your estate agent? ☐

Have you decided on sole agency or multi-agency? ☐

Have you negotiated on their terms and conditions? ☐

Have you expressed an interest in floor plans and photos? ☐

Have you agreed the asking price? ☐

Have you given the agent your solicitor's details? ☐

Have you checked through the details/brochure to make sure that everything is correct? ☐

Are you sure that your property is realistically priced? ☐

Presentation

Have you sorted out all your possessions? ☐

Have you finished all those little DIY jobs? ☐

Have you de-cluttered all of the rooms? ☐

Have you repainted where necessary? ☐

Will you be painting the front door? ☐

Is the garden presentable? ☐

Are the outside of the house, the gate, the pathway presentable? ☐

Is your house number or name clearly visible? ☐

Have you thoroughly cleaned the kitchen and bathroom? ☐

Do you need to hire professional cleaners? ☐

Do you need a handyman to help with finishing little jobs? ☐

Have you told the estate agents that you're not ready for viewings until everything is finished? ☐

Have you created as much space and light as possible? ☐

Have you changed all the light bulbs? ☐

On the market

Are you ready for viewings? ☐

Have you given keys to the estate agent to do viewings in your absence? ☐

If you are showing the property yourself, have you got all the information at your fingertips? ☐

Have you arranged for somebody to look after your children/pets while you are conducting viewings? ☐

Are you presenting your property immaculately? ☐

Have you suggested to your agent that you have an open day? ☐

If you are unhappy with the lack of viewings, have you thought about changing agents? ☐

Are you in constant touch with your agent? ☐

If the property is 'sticking', what are you going to do about it? ☐

Do you need to market your property in a different way? ☐

Are you advertising it on various internet sites, as well as your agent's? ☐

The offer

Are you prepared to negotiate when you receive an offer? ☐

Is the offer realistic? ☐

Are you prepared to negotiate on fixtures and fittings? ☐

Have you filled in the fixtures and fittings form? ☐

Are you ready to exchange contracts? ☐

Do you need a delayed completion? ☐

Are your finances in place regarding the next property? ☐

Having accepted an offer subject to contract, do you
want a memorandum of sale or a small deposit from
the buyer to show their intent? ☐

Are you in regular contact with your solicitor? ☐

Have you agreed a date to exchange contracts? ☐

Have you chosen a date for completion? ☐

Are you getting ready for the move?(Now turn to
Chapter 9.) ☐

The Big Move

CHAPTER 9

Moving

Choosing your removal company

Preparing for the move

Countdown to the move

Who to notify before you move

Top tips for staying sane

Everyone knows that moving house is one of life's most stressful experiences and yet it needn't be. You need to be prepared and organised and retain a sense of humour for everything to be plain sailing. Not all of us, however, are prepared and organised, which is why it all becomes so stressful.

As a little girl I moved home dozens of times because my father was in the British Army. My mother became an accomplished house-mover and would have our new home looking straight within three days, with pictures on the walls and everything put away. So I suppose I had a useful training in how to move home painlessly.

Choosing your removal company

Remember, no two house moves are the same, so the removal company will send out an estimator to assess the quantity of possessions you have, the amount of packing, the distance the van or vans will have to travel, the number of removal men involved, which floor you live on if it is a flat, and any other requirements, and will base their quote on that information. You should get three quotes to make sure you get the best value (sometimes the famous names are the most reasonable), and make sure you show them the contents of the attic, garage and garden shed. These are often forgotten and will affect the quote.

When choosing your removal company make sure they are a member of the BAR. The British Association of Removers (see Useful Addresses) is a regulatory body that imposes certain regulations on its members to do with insurance, training and code of conduct. If your company is not with the BAR make sure they have the necessary insurance to cover any damages.

Most removal companies will offer a range of services and it is important that you make clear what you require.

- **A standard move** – this is basically DIY where the removal company supply all the boxes, paper, bubble wrap etc., but you do all the packing. The company will then load, travel and unload.

- **Fragile packing** – the removers pack all the breakables only, but you do the rest. They then load the van, travel and unload.

- **Full packing service** – they will literally do everything, including your clothes. They pack, load, travel, unload and unpack.

- **Combination service** – this is what I usually have and it depends on the individual household. They will do a complete packing service, load, travel, unload the boxes and leave them packed. Or unpack some. It depends what state your new house is in! It may not be ready to unpack everything. They will distribute the furniture and boxes into rooms as directed and then leave.

- **Storage** – you can have everything loaded into a container and stored for you while you are looking for something to buy. Alternatively, you could do part move/part storage. During the estimate make sure the remover knows which pieces are going where – coloured stickers help – because this will affect the quote.

> If you are selling some furniture prior to moving, make sure you tell the assessor because it could make all the difference between needing one container and two.

Removers will also provide special services for antiques and pianos, if they are needed. The really good removal companies have people who know exactly how to protect antiques and will call in expert carpenters to take apart antique wardrobes or dressers. These are then reassembled at the other end. They have sophisticated pulley systems to get furniture out of top-floor windows and experts who deal with unwiring and packing chandeliers. No problem is insurmountable. Whatever your needs, however humble or grand, they've seen it all before and are there to help you.

Once you have received your three quotes it is up to you to decide who will do the job. I usually go for the middle quote. When you have accepted their quote make sure you get it all confirmed in writing. You will need to tell them your moving date but if your house is still going through legal negotiations and you have not agreed a completion date, you could always give them a provisional booking. Do this as far in advance as possible. In fact, I usually get the removal people in to quote before the house is even on the market.

Keep in close contact with them so that you can confirm the moving date as soon as possible (i.e. as soon as contracts have been exchanged).

The cost of moving

- The cost of your move will depend on a variety of factors and not just how much stuff you have got. The assessor has to take these factors into account.

- The cubic capacity required to pack all your belongings. This will affect the number of vans you will need.

- Which service you require. If they are doing a full pack it can take three men five days to pack, depending on the size of the property.

- Access. If your home is on the fourth floor without a lift or the van can't park near your house it will affect the price.

- The timing. Fridays, weekends, school holidays and the last week of the month are really bad times to move. Removal companies are stretched to the limits, so you may not receive the best service.

- The amount of packaging.

- The distance the van has to travel and how long to unload/unpack. This sometimes means an overnight stay for the lads.

- Storage. The cubic capacity will affect the weekly rental.

TOP TIPS

Here are my three top tips for avoiding a stressful move.

1. The summer holiday season is a crazy time to move. Removal men like to take their children on holiday too, so many companies employ casual labour at such times.

2. Confirm the time when the keys to the new house are available and who pays for any waiting time. The people leaving the new house might be doing it themselves and take longer than anticipated, which leaves your company waiting for them to finish.

3. Always check if your move will be a part load. (This means more than one job on the van.) If a job is cancelled or delayed it could stop the whole job taking place.

CHECKLIST

Choosing your removal company checklist

Get three quotes. ☐

Show the assessors everything including the attic, garden shed and garage. ☐

Show them all garden pots, statues and furniture that are going. ☐

Make sure they are with the BAR (or well insured if not). ☐

Check the small print in the quote to make sure that VAT, insurance and packing materials are included. There should be no hidden extras. ☐

Discuss the range of services and tell them what you need. Each move is different, so go ahead and ask questions. ☐

Tell them about any furniture that is not going on the van. ☐

Once you have accepted a quote, get it in writing. ☐

Book your moving date. (Try to avoid weekends.) ☐

If things go wrong or you are behind on the packing let them know. The dates can change but you must keep in touch. ☐

Use coloured stickers if some of your possessions are going into storage. ☐

Agree a time when they can start packing. Sometimes this is days before the move. ☐

After you have had your massive clear-out, decide which things should go to the charity shops, as they will be more than grateful to receive clothes, jewellery and bric-a-brac. The Salvation Army will even collect small items of furniture. Other stuff that you feel has some monetary value could always go to a car boot sale, but I always think that these are an awful lot of work for a minimum return. Do you need the extra stress?

CASE STUDY

Brian and Lesley Dorling were moving into a house only a few streets away from their present home in York. They hired a removal company to do the packing and loading on the day of completion. They were in a chain, so on that day eight people were moving from one home to another and the Dorlings had to be out by 2 p.m. to let their buyers in.

They had been told that their load would be a part load, meaning they would be sharing the van with a couple moving out of York.

By 9 o'clock on the morning of the move the van still hadn't arrived, when they were expecting it at 7.00 a.m. Mr Dorling was told that the van had broken down and was on its way. By 12 noon it still hadn't arrived. He rang the removal company again and was told that the other part load had been delayed and they wouldn't be able to do his job at all.

By now his hair had begun to turn grey and he knew there would be a penalty if his house was not ready for occupation by 2 p.m. So he made three calls. He rang his insurers, his solicitor and the BAR.

His solicitor was able to warn the buyers that there was a problem and negotiate a delay. His insurance company said they would cover him – for a small extra premium – against any claim for the inconvenience and delay to the completion and the BAR were able to recommend a removal company in the area who could do the job at the last minute. By the following day the problem had been solved but the knock-on effect to other people was horrendous. The moral? In an ideal world do not agree to be part of a load.

Preparing for the move

Option 1: They do it all

You have a choice, either you do it or they do it. Obviously, it will cost more if they do it all but if you have a job and a family, there aren't enough hours in the day to start packing bits of china. What price sanity? They are all very good at their job, so let them do it. One removal chap I spoke to said that he actually prefers it if the customer leaves it all to them. 'You don't have to move a thing. Leave the pictures on the walls and the china in the cupboards so that the boxes can be labelled accordingly.'

They will pack all your clothes and hanging garments will be transported in mobile wardrobe boxes. It couldn't be easier. Your biggest contribution will be in the preparation and you can never start soon enough. Clear out all the junk which has been accumulating over the years. You don't want to start life in your new house surrounded by clutter.

It would be very helpful if you could draw a little plan of your new home, giving each room a name or number. If you give this to the removal company they will make sure all the boxes go into the right rooms. Ideally, you should be there on the day in order to make quick decisions and to make sure everything is where you want it.

I usually pack all my personal bits and pieces such as office files, jewellery and make-up etc. Here is a list of essentials that should travel with you and not on the van:

CHECKLIST

Checklist for what should travel with you

Kettle ☐

Tea/coffee, milk and sugar ☐

Soft drinks for children ☐

Washing-up liquid and cleaning materials ☐

Sheets, duvets and towels ☐

Change of clothes ☐

Mobile phone ☐

Washing things and soap ☐

Loo roll ☐

Emergency rations like snack food, bread, butter, cereal ☐

Children's things (toys, nappies, food) ☐

Plastic cups or china mugs ☐

Make sure the vacuum cleaner is the first thing off the van! ☐

This way, when you get to your destination you won't be waiting for essentials to come off the van. They will then start to unload and unpack everything, so make them lots of cups of tea (they will need lots of tea during packing as well), so you might need to get in some extra milk and sugar.

Keep calm. Most removal men have a lovely sense of humour so the banter will help to keep you relaxed. If they are doing it all, you can get on with making the beds etc. They will assemble everything and put furniture wherever you want it. (They will even carry heavy garden pots across the garden and place them where you want them.)

Different coloured sticky labels are an absolute godsend. If you are sending some furniture into storage, some to the new house and some to your parents, as I once did, you will need three different colours in order to assist the removal men.

Option 2: You do it yourself

Well, you're very brave. This is quite the most stressful way of doing it but of course it is the cheapest. Also, if you are very minimalist and don't have much stuff then it makes sense to do it yourself.

If you don't need a professional removal company you could always hire a van, pack the boxes, get a friend to help you load up and drive it yourself. Ring around for quotes on the van hire and make sure it includes insurance and breakdown cover. However, you need to be strong to do it yourself as some boxes will be quite heavy. A friend or two will be needed to help you and you will need to have pre-packed all the boxes prior to the moving day. Self-drive vans for hire can be found in the *Yellow Pages*.

Alternatively, you could hire a van with a driver, which will cost a bit more. Ask the driver whether he will help with the loading and if he has all the equipment such as packing blankets and ropes. Always check his insurance.

If you *are* using a removal firm but are doing all the packing yourself, here is a list of things to help you prepare.

CHECKLIST

Doing it yourself checklist

Book removal firm early. ☐

Plan ahead. Make lists of things to do. This helps prevent sleepless nights. ☐

Clear out all the unwanted items. ☐

Get packing materials delivered early. (You can never start too soon.) ☐

Start packing. All china and glass should be packed singly. Don't overload boxes. Put heavy items at the bottom and light at the top. □

Put books in small boxes otherwise you won't be able to lift them. □

Label each box clearly, stating the contents. You could also put which room they are intended for. □

Pack pictures back to back and face to face in large boxes. Pad out any gaps. □

Use wardrobe boxes for hanging garments. □

Clothing in drawers can stay where they are. □

You will need plenty of sticky tape and several large felt pens. □

Get an electrician to dismantle wall lights (if you are taking them). □

Remember to let everyone know your change of address. □

Remember to pack a bag with overnight things. (See checklist on page 198.) □

Leave the vacuum cleaner out until last because you will want to have a quick flash about before you leave. (You'll be shocked by what you find under the beds.) □

See the BAR (British Association of Removers) checklist below for all other reminders. □

On the following page is a checklist provided by the BAR.

Later on (see pages 203–5), you will see that I have broken this down as a countdown to the move.

CHECKLIST

BAR checklist

Confirm dates with the mover. ☐

Sign and return contract together with payment. ☐

Book insurance at declared value. ☐

Arrange a contact number. ☐

Dispose of anything you don't want. ☐

Start running down freezer contents. ☐

Contact carpet fitters if needed. ☐

Book mains services for disconnection. ☐

Cancel all rental agreements. ☐

Notify doctor, dentist, optician, vet. ☐

Tell your bank and savings/share accounts. ☐

Inform telephone company. ☐

Ask Post Office to re-route mail. ☐

Tell TV licence, car registration, passport offices of address changes. ☐

Notify hire purchase (HP) and credit firms. ☐

Make local map to new house for friends and moving company. ☐

Clear the loft. ☐

Organise parking at new home (for removal van). ☐

Plan where things go in new home. ☐

Cancel the milk/newspapers. ☐

Clean out the freezer. ☐

Arrange minders for children/pets. ☐

Find and label keys. ☐

Address cards to friends and relatives. ☐

Separate trinkets, jewellery and small items. ☐

Sort out linen and clothes. ☐

Put garage/garden tools together. ☐

Take down curtains/blinds. ☐

Collect children's toys. ☐

Put together basic catering for family at new house. ☐

Countdown to the move

Four weeks before the move

CHECKLIST

Have a big sort out and chuck out all the junk. ☐

Check that your home contents insurance covers you for the move. ☐

Have you got insurance for your new home? ☐

Arrange for gas and electricity to be disconnected. ☐

Let your telephone company know when to disconnect. ☐

Start collecting cardboard boxes and packaging materials. ☐

Get quotes from three different removal companies. ☐

Make sure they are well insured. ☐

Once you've chosen your company give them your moving
address, telephone number at new address, possible date and
any other instructions. ☐

One week before the move

CHECKLIST

Phone the removal company to confirm the date and time of
your move. ☐

Arrange for your mail to be redirected. ☐

Start defrosting your freezer. ☐

Cancel the milk, newspapers etc. ☐

Notify your friends, family and utilities of your new address. ☐

Start packing if you are doing it yourself. ☐

Make notes or a little map of the new property, so you know
where everything is to go. ☐

Pack a few essentials in a separate box. ☐

Label all boxes clearly. ☐

Keep the hoover, dustpan and brush, and a few cleaning
materials handy. ☐

One day before the move

CHECKLIST

Pack an overnight case with essentials. (See page 198.) ☐

Defrost fridge. ☐

Arrange for someone to take care of the children and pets. ☐

Make sure you have some cash. ☐

Order a takeaway. ☐

Who to notify before your move

Remember to arrange for any mail to be forwarded to your new address. This can be done by the Post Office for a small fee and can be for a period of one month to a year and extended if necessary.

I always print out 'change of address' cards on the computer because it is so much quicker, and cheaper, than the printers. Make sure your old address is on it as well as the new address and telephone number for all the organisations that need to know, such as:

- your bank or building society;

- the Inland Revenue;

- National Insurance;

- credit card companies and any hire purchase agreements you may have;

- social security office for pensions or benefits;

- local authority re council tax;

- water authority;

- your insurance company re contents and buildings insurance;

- life insurance etc.;

- health insurer, if any;

- doctor, dentist, hospital, clinic;

- DVLC regarding your vehicle registration and driving licence;

- motor insurers;

- AA or RAC;

- schools, clubs or organisations that you belong to;

- the library;

- any other mailing lists;

- VAT office;

- TV licence office;

- your union or association;

- pension fund;

- friends, colleagues, neighbours and relatives.

What to do the other end

I am very much in favour of making lists. Writing everything down really helps both you and/or the removal men to know where everything goes. With your list in your hot little hand you should be able to unload the van in a trice.

So, you're in your new home. On the first night I'd try not to get too ambitious because you'll only end up knackered. Once the beds have arrived, make them up and sort out your personal belongings. You may need to give the bathroom a quick clean. If you have children, make sure their bedrooms are sorted.

TOP TIPS

Here are my three top tips for reducing stress once you arrive in your new home.

1. If the removal men are unloading but *not* unpacking, store everything in room-by-room sections, so that you can find the right box quickly. All the kitchen stuff together etc. Write the contents on the side of the box (the men usually write contents on the top), so that when they are stacked you can easily see what is inside.

2. Loud music is a great stress reliever. You might as well accept that it is going to be a bit chaotic for a while and this will help to keep you calm.

3. Delegating little jobs is vital because you can't do them all yourself.

The next day you can really get cracking. Try to set yourself targets and this will motivate you. For example, 'Today I'm going to finish the sitting room'. When we moved I decided to do our bedroom first. It is very important to get one room straight, as a haven that you can retreat to, to get away from all the mess.

Slowly but surely you will see the boxes disappearing. Try to unpack as much as you can every day because the sooner your home is straight the better. This helps your peace of mind and enables you to channel your energy elsewhere. A chaotic home often means a chaotic mind. Clutter and mess are not conducive to harmony and stability.

Unless you are having building work done, like we were, there is no reason why your home shouldn't be unpacked and finished within two weeks (I'm serious). That includes pictures on the walls and everything! Honestly, you will feel so much better if you keep going until it is all done rather than putting it off for another day.

If you need shelves to put all your books on, get a handyman or carpenter in right away. Ask around. There is bound to be someone who can help you. It might be useful to locate a plumber as well, in case of an emergency.

If, after two years, you still have boxes that remain unpacked, get rid of them. You obviously haven't missed the contents.

CHECKLIST

Arrival checklist

Make up the beds first. ☐

Settle the children's rooms. ☐

Unpack a little and often. ☐

Store boxes room by room. ☐

Delegate. ☐

Set yourself targets. ☐

Organise your bedroom quickly. ☐

Get a handyman to help with shelves etc. ☐

Keep going until it is finished. ☐

TOP TIPS

Here are my 16 top tips to help you stay sane during the big move.

1. Make lots of lists prior to the move because if you try to remember everything it will cause sleepless nights. Your brain will be working overtime, so I've found that last thing at night I would make a list of 'things to do tomorrow'. This allows the brain to rest. Also, use the BAR and my checklists and tick them off as you go along.

2. Be ruthless with your possessions. I found that getting rid of a lot of our 'stuff' – particularly the stuff that we didn't need – was immensely liberating and cathartic. If you find it hard to decide whether you need it or not, try this little test. Is it useful? Does it have a function? Is it aesthetically pleasing? If it is a toasted sandwich maker that doesn't work but you said you'd fix it two years ago, then chuck it out.

3. Never look back. Leaving a home is bound to be an emotional experience, particularly if you have very fond memories of it. But you should be looking to the future and not dwelling on the past. Be optimistic at all times.

4. If you are packing up yourself, get some friends round with some wine and beers and make a party of it. It can be great fun.

5. Ask a friend or neighbour to make supper for you and the family the night before the move. (You won't be able to find any saucepans.) Or get a takeaway.

6. One of my biggest tips for staying sane during the move (and sometimes the build-up to the move) is to have children and pets taken care of. Ask family or friends to look after them for you because you need to be hands-free on the day.

7. Children are unsettled by a move and can become demanding when you least need them to be. Once you arrive, involve them in their new home as much as possible by allowing them to unpack their own belongings and to even decorate their own rooms.

8. Take some cleaning materials with you in the car. Once the van has departed you will set off to your destination and probably arrive first. The last time you saw that kitchen it probably looked fine, but now that it's empty it may need a quick clean.

9. Alternatively, book a cleaning company well in advance of completion. Get the agents to hand the keys to the cleaners. After a few hours you can move into a spotless home.

10. If something is broken during the move, don't get angry or stressed. You are covered by their insurance and most things can be fixed anyway. If it can't be fixed, well, so what? I'm of the opinion that we attach too much importance to possessions.

11. Register with the local doctor as soon as possible. Especially if you have children.

12. Coloured sticky labels will be immensely helpful.

13. Be nice to the removal men and they will do anything for you. (Especially if you're a girl!)

14. Don't be afraid to ask questions, whether it be to the removal company, the estate agent, your solicitor, the previous owner, the vet. They are all there to help you and understand how stressful the move can be.

16. Don't put off until tomorrow what you can do today. I'm afraid it's so true prior to a move. The days will fly by and watching television won't get anything done. I found that the more I did, the more energy I had.

Enjoy your new home. Look after it and it will look after you.

Conclusion

Some of us are natural home-makers and nest-builders and some of us are not. But it really doesn't matter whether it looks like a cosy, cookies-in-the-oven sort of home or a functional space where you lay your head, as long as you remember a few basic rules.

- When you set out to buy your property the location is of paramount importance.

- You don't pay over its market value otherwise you will be shaving your profit when you sell.

- You do your research.

- If you are undertaking improvements, you do them really well, as suggested in this book. And finally…

- When you sell, you get the timing and the presentation right.

This way you should see the financial rewards of buying and selling, and will be shooting up the property ladder.

Glossary

Here are some terms you may come across in connection with conveyancing, insurance or arranging a mortgage.

Advance The mortgage loan (*also* Capital sum, Principal sum).

All-risks insurance Insurance that covers everything that is not specifically excluded in the policy.

APR Annual Percentage Rates: the standard way of working out the true interest rate; the APR has to be shown by banks and building societies alongside their quoted rates for each mortgage, to enable potential borrowers to compare equally what is being offered.

Assignment The transfer of ownership to another person including property, insurance policies or a lease.

Balance outstanding The amount of loan owed at any one time.

Bonus Additional amounts paid on a policy.

Bridging loan Yuk! A loan, usually from a bank, at very high interest rates to enable you to buy a house when you have been unable to sell your own.

Capital The mortgage loan (also called the advance).

Capital-reducing mortgage Repayment mortgage.

Charges Register One of the three registers maintained by the Land Registry for a property. It records interests adverse to the owner.

Completion date The day when the money is paid, the deeds are handed over, the keys are released and you can move into your house.

Conditions of sale The terms in the contract as stipulated by a buyer or seller to which he will agree to buy/sell the house.

Contract The agreement to sell the property. Not binding until exchange of contracts.

Conveyance A written document transferring unregistered land from the seller to the buyer.

Conveyancing The legal process involved in transferring the ownership of land or property from one owner to another.

Covenant A promise in a deed to undertake (if covenant is positive) or not do (if restrictive covenant) specified things.

Creditor Someone such as the lender who is owed money.

Differentials When extra interest is charged on larger loans; these are known as differentials.

Early redemption Paying off a loan before the end of the mortgage term.

Early redemption charge The sum charged by a lender in the event of a loan being paid off before the end of the mortgage term. This is sometimes known as a penalty payment.

Easement A legal term meaning the use of another person's land – for example, a pathway across your neighbour's property.

Endowment policy An investment that can be linked to a mortgage loan to pay off the capital at the end of the term (or on death, if sooner).

Endowment mortgage A loan on which only interest is paid throughout the term; linked to an endowment policy.

Exchange of contracts When the agreement to buy or sell your house becomes legally binding.

Freehold The property and the land on which it sits will belong to you or your dependants indefinitely.

Indemnity covenant This is a clause in the contract in which the buyer agrees to take on any responsibility or legal obligations that the seller may have had.

Index map search A search to find out if ownership of a property is registered at the Land Registry.

Joint tenants or tenants in common When two or more people co-own a property, if one were to die, his or her share would automatically pass to the other.

Land Certificate A certificate issued by the Land Registry to confirm the ownership of a house.

Land Registry The government department responsible for maintaining and amending the registration of all properties in England and Wales that have registered titles.

Leasehold The ownership of a property for a fixed number of years, granted by the freeholder.

Lessee A person who takes a lease (i.e. the tenant).

Lessor A person who grants a lease (i.e. the landlord).

Local search certificate An application made to the local authority for a certificate providing certain information about a property and the surrounding area.

Low-start mortgage A loan for which premiums start low and increase by a certain percentage each year until the full level premium is reached.

Mortgage A loan for which your house is the security or collateral. It gives to your lender the right to sell the property if the mortgage payments are not made.

Mortgage deed The document stating the conditions of your loan.

Mortgagee The lender.

Mortgage protection policy insurance (MPPI) An extra form of life insurance taken out by the borrower in case of death or illness.

Mortgagor The borrower.

Office copy (entries) A copy of your Land Registry documents. The term also applies to other official copies – such as probates or letters of administration.

Preliminary enquiries The questions asked about a property before exchange of contracts.

Premium A monthly or one-off payment for an insurance policy.

Principal The amount of money that has been borrowed and on which interest is calculated.

Proprietorship Register Part of the Land Certificate that records the names of the owners and any restrictions on their right to sell.

Redemption Paying off the loan at the end of the term.

Registered land Land that is registered at the Land Registry.

Repayment mortgage Loan on which the capital as well as interest is paid back throughout the period of the loan.

Requisitions on title These are questions asked about the seller's ownership of the land and any matters raised before completion.

Retention A mortgage company will withhold part of your loan if you are carrying out extensive renovations or building a brand new house. They sometimes pay in instalments depending on how well the work is progressing.

Stakeholder Someone who will hold the deposit as an intermediary between the buyer and seller. This is usually your solicitor.

'Subject to contract' These words should appear in every letter to the seller or his solicitor before contracts are exchanged. This is to protect the buyer in case it all goes wrong.

Surrender value The amount of money a policyholder receives if a life insurance policy is terminated before the expiry date (other than on death).

Term of mortgage The number of years at the end of which the loan is to be repaid.

Title The right to ownership of property.

Title deeds The documents conferring the ownership of land or property.

Top-up mortgage Additional mortgage from another lender when the first lender does not provide enough finance to purchase a house.

Transfer The Land Registry document transferring the ownership of the property from the seller to the buyer.

Unit-linked policy A life insurance policy under which the premiums buy units in an investment fund.

Vendor The seller.

Warranty A guarantee to accept responsibility for necessary repairs over a specified period such as provided by the NHBC.

Useful Addresses

Architects' Registration Council of the United Kingdom
73 Hallam Street,
London W1N 5LQ
Tel: 020 7580 5861   Fax: 020 7436 5269

The Architectural Association
34–36 Bedford Square,
London WC1B 3ES
Tel: 020 7887 4000   Fax: 020 7414 0782
Email: arch-assoc@arch-assoc.org.uk
Website: www.arch-assoc.org.uk

The Architecture and Surveying Institute (ASI)
St Mary House,
15A St Mary Street,
Chippenham,
Wiltshire SN15 3WD
Tel: 01249 444505   Fax: 01249 443602. Email: mail@asi.org.uk
Website: www.asi.org.uk

The Association of British Insurers
51–55 Gresham Street,
London EC2V 7HQ

Tel: 020 7600 3333   Fax: 020 7696 8999 Email: info@abi.org.uk
Website: www.abi.org.uk

The Association of Building Engineers (ABE)
Lutyens House,
Billing Brook Road,
Weston Favell,
Northamptonshire NN3 8NW
Tel: 01604 404121   Fax: 01604 784 220
Email: buildengrs@aol.com

The Association of Plumbing and Heating Contractors (APHC)
14 Ensign House,
Ensign Business Centre,
Westwood Way,
Coventry CV4 8JA
Tel: 02476 470626   Fax: 02476 470942.
Email: aphuk@aol.com   Website: www.licensedplumber.co.uk

Association of Relocation Agents
PO Box 189,
Diss, Norfolk IP22 1PE
Tel: 08700 737 475   Fax 01359 251508
Email info@relocationagents.com
Website: www.relocationagents.com

Association of Residential Letting Agents
ARLA Administration,
Maple House,
53–55 Woodside Road,
Amersham,
Bucks HP6 6AA
Tel: 01494 431680   Website: www.arla.co.uk

The British Association of Removers (BAR)
3 Churchill Court,
58 Station Road,
North Harrow,
Middlesex HA2 7SA.
Tel: 020 8861 3331   Fax: 020 8861 3332   Email: info@bar.co.uk
Website: www.barmovers.com

The British Insurance Brokers' Association (BIBA)
BIBA House,
14 Bevis Marks,
London EC3A 7NT
Tel: 020 7623 9043   Fax: 020 7626 9676
Email: enquiries@biba.org.uk   Website: www.biba.org.uk

The British Wood Preserving and Damp-proofing Association
6 The Office Village,
4 Romford Road,
London E15 4EA
Tel: 020 8519 2588   Fax: 020 8519 3444
Email: info@bwpda.co.uk   Website: www.bwpda.co.uk

***Build It* Magazine**
Inside Communications,
The Isis Building,
Thames Quay,
193 Marsh Wall
London E14 9SG
Tel: 020 7772 8300   Fax: 020 7772 8584
Website: www.self-build.co.uk

Builders' Merchants Federation
15 Soho Square,
London W1V 5FB
Tel: 020 7439 1753

Building Employers' Confederation
66 Cardiff Road,
Glan Y Llyn,
Cardiff CF15 7PQ
Tel: 029 2081 0681

The Building Societies Association (BSA)
3 Savile Row,
London W1Z 1AF
Tel: 020 7437 0655   Fax: 020 7734 6416
Website: www.bsa.org.uk

Cadw (Welsh Heritage)
Cathays Park,
Cardiff CF10 3NQ
Tel: 02920 500 200

Chartered Institute of Building Services Engineers
Delta House,
22 Balham High Road,
London SW12 9BS
Tel: 020 8675 5211

The Construction Federation
Construction House,
56–64 Leonard Street,
London EC2A 4JX
Tel: 020 7608 5000   Fax: 020 7608 5001
Email: enquiries@theCC.org.uk   Website: www.theCC.org.uk

Consumers' Association
2 Marylebone Road,
London NW1 4DF
Tel: 020 7830 6000

Corgi (The Council for Registered Gas Installers)
4 Elmwood,
Chineham Business Park,
Crockford Lane,
Basingstoke,
Hampshire RG24 8WG
Tel: 01256 372200   Website: www.corgi-gas.co.uk

The Corporation of Insurance, Financial and Mortgage Advisors (CIFMA)
174 High Street,
Guildford,
Surrey GU1 3HW
Tel: 01483 539121   Fax: 01483 301847.

Council for Licensed Conveyancers (CLC)
16 Glebe Road,
Chelmsford,
Essex CM1 1QG
Tel: 01245 349599   Fax: 01245 341300.
Email: conveyancer@conveyancer.org.uk
Website: www.conveyancer.org.uk

The Council of Mortgage Lenders
3 Savile Row,
London W1X 1AF
Tel: 020 7440 2255   Fax: 020 7434 3791
Website: www.cml.org.uk

Department of the Environment, Transport and the Regions
Eland House,
Bressenden Place,
London SW1 5DU
Tel: 020 7890 3000   Website: www.detr.gov.uk

The Electrical Contractors' Association
ESCA House,
34 Palace Court,
Bayswater,
London W2 4HY
Tel: 020 7313 4800

The Electrical Contractors' Association of Scotland
Bush House,
Bush Estate,
Midlothian EH26 0SB
Tel: 0131 445 5577   Fax: 0131 445 5548   Email: ecas@fol.co.uk
Website: www.select.org.uk

English Heritage
23 Savile Row,
London, W1S 2ET
Tel: 020 7973 3000   Website: www.english-heritage.org.uk

Federation of Cable Services
Keswick House,
207 Anerley Road,
London SE20 8ER
Tel: 020 8778 5656   Fax: 020 8778 8402   Email: fcs@fcs.org.uk
Website: www.fcs.org.uk

The Federation of Master Builders
Gordon Fisher House,
14–15 Great James Street,
London WC1N 3DP
Tel: 020 7242 7583   Fax: 020 7242 0505
Website: www.fmb.org.uk

Fire Protection Association
Melrose Avenue,
Boreham Wood,
Herts WD6 2BJ
Tel: 020 8236 9700

The Georgian Group
6 Fitzroy Square,
London W1T 5DX
Tel: 020 7529 8920

Glass and Glazing Federation
44–48 Borough High Street,
London SE1 1XB
Tel: 020 7403 7177   Fax: 020 7357 7458

The Guarantee Protection Trust
27 London Road,
High Wycombe,
Bucks HP11 1BW
Tel: 01494 447049   Fax: 01494 465194
Email shirley@gptprotection.co.uk
Website: www.gptprotection.co.uk

Guild of Master Craftsmen
Prest House,
Exelby,
Bedale,
North Yorks DL8 2HB
Tel: 01677 427183

The Heating and Ventilating Contractors' Association (HVCA)
ESCA House,
34 Palace Court,
London W2 4JG

Tel: 020 7313 4900   Fax: 020 7727 9268
Email: contact@hvca.org.uk   Website: www.hvca.org.uk

Historic Scotland
133 Longmore House,
Salisbury Place,
Edinburgh EH9 1SH
Tel: 0131 668 8600

HM Land Registry Headquarters
Lincoln's Inn Fields,
London WC2A 3PH
Tel: 020 7917 8888   Fax: 020 7955 0110

Home Buyer Legal Protection Ltd
8 Broad Street,
Wokingham,
Berkshire RG40 1AB
Tel: 0118 989 0914

The Housing Corporation
149 Tottenham Court Road,
London W1P 0BN
Tel: 020 7393 2000   Fax: 020 7393 2111
Website: www.housingcorp.gov.uk

The Independent Schools Information Service (ISIS)
Grosvenor Gardens House,
35–37 Grosvenor Gardens,
London SW1W 0BS
Tel: 020 7798 1500   Fax: 020 7798 1501
Email: national@isis.org.uk   Website: www.isis.org.uk

Institute of Electrical Engineers
Savoy Place,
London WC2R 0BL
Tel: 020 7240 1871

The Institute of Plumbing
64 Station Lane,
Hornchurch,
Essex RM12 6NB
Tel: 01708 472791

The Lands Tribunal for Scotland
1 Grosvenor Crescent,
Edinburgh EH12 5ER
Tel: 0131 225 7996   Fax: 0131 226 4812

The Law Commission
Conquest House,
37–38 John Street,
Theobalds Road,
London WC1N 2BQ.
Tel: 020 7453 1220   Fax: 020 7453 1297
Email: secretary.lawcomm@gtnet.gov.uk
Website: www.lawcom.gov.uk

The Law Society
113 Chancery Lane,
London WC2A 1PL
Tel: 020 7242 1222   Fax: 020 7831 0344.
Website: www.lawsociety.org.uk

The Law Society (Scotland)
26 Drumsheugh Gardens,
Edinburgh EH3 7YR
Tel: 0131 226 7411   Helpline: 0131 476 8137

Fax: 0131 225 2934   Email: lawscot@lawscot.org.uk
Website: www.lawscot.org.uk

Legal Services Ombudsman
22 Oxford Court,
Oxford Street,
Manchester M2 3WQ
Tel: 0161 236 9532   Fax: 0161 236 2651
Email: enquiries.olso@gtnet.gov.uk

Listed Property Owners Club
FREEPOST
Hartlip,
Sittingbourne,
Kent ME9 7TE
Tel: 01795 844939
Email: info@listedpropertyownersclub.co.uk

The Location Company
1 Charlotte Street,
London W1T 1RB
Tel: 020 7637 7766   Website: www.thelocation.co.uk

National Approved Letting Scheme
PO Box 1843,
Warwick CV34 4ZA
Tel: 01926 496683   Website: www.nalscheme.co.uk

National Association of Citizens' Advice Bureaux
80–82 St John's Road,
Tunbridge Wells,
Kent TN 4 9PH
Tel: 01892 539275

The National Association of Estate Agents
Arbon House,
21 Jury Street,
Warwick CV34 4EH
Tel: 01926 496800   Fax: 01926 400953
Email: naea@dial.pipex.com   Website: www.naea.co.uk

National Conservatory Advisory Council
NRWAS,
PO Box 163,
Bangor,
County Down BT20 5BX
Tel: 0500 522525   Website: www.nrwas.com

National Federation of Roofing Contractors Limited
24 Weymouth Street,
London, W1N 4LX
Tel: 020 7436 0387   Fax: 020 7637 5215

The National Guild of Removers and Storers
22a High Street,
Chesham,
Bucks HP5 1EP
Tel: 01494 792279   Fax: 01494 792111
Website: www.ngrs.co.uk

The National House Building Council (NHBC)
NHBC, Buildmark House,
Chiltern Avenue,
Amersham,
Bucks HP6 5AP
Tel: 0845 845 6422   Website: www.nhbc.co.uk

National Home Improvement Advisory Service
NHIAS,
The Mount,
2 Woodstock Link,
Belfast BT6 8DD
Tel: 0800 0851 246   Website: www.nhias.org

The National Inspection Council for Electrical Installation Contracting (NICEIC)
Vintage House,
37 Albert Embankment,
London SE1 7UJ
Tel: 020 7564 2323   Fax: 020 7564 2370
Website: www.niceic.org.uk

National Register of Warranted Builders
Gordon Fisher House,
14–15 Great James Street,
London WC1N 3DP
Tel: 020 7404 4155

The New Home Marketing Board (NHMB)
56–64 Leonard Street,
London EC2A 4JX
Tel: 020 7608 5100   Fax: 020 7608 5101
Email: mca@wof.co.uk   Website: www.wof.co.uk

Northern Ireland Housing Executive
The Housing Centre,
2 Adelaide Street,
Belfast BT2 8PB
Tel: 01232 317000   Website: www.nihe.gov.uk

Office of Fair Trading
Field House,
15–25 Bream's Buildings,
London EC4A 1PR
Tel: 020 7211 8000

Office of the Ombudsman for Estate Agents
Beckett House,
4 Bridge Street,
Salisbury,
Wiltshire SP1 2LX
Tel: 01722 333306   Fax: 01722 332296
Email: post@oea.co.uk   Website: www.oea.co.uk

Office for the Supervision of Solicitors
Victoria Court,
8 Dormer Place,
Leamington Spa,
Warwickshire CV32 5AE
Tel: 01926 820082   Fax: 01926 431435
Website: www.lawsociety.org.uk

The Pre-School Learning Alliance (PLA)
69 King's Cross Road,
London WC1X 9LL
Tel: 020 7833 0991   Fax: 020 7837 4942.
Email: pla@preschool.org.uk

Railtrack Property
26 Southwark Street,
London SE1 1TU
Tel: 020 7645 3000   Fax: 7645 3001

Registry of County Court Judgments
Registry Trust Ltd,
173–175 Cleveland Street,
London W1P 5PE
Tel: 020 7380 0133

The Royal Incorporation of Architects in Scotland (RIA Scotland)
15 Rutland Square,
Edinburgh EH1 2BE
Tel: 0131 229 7205

Clients' Advisory Service: 0131 229 7545 Fax: 0131 228 2188.
Website: www.rias.org.uk

The Royal Institute of British Architects
66 Portland Place,
London W1B 1AD
Tel: 020 7580 5533   Website: www.architecture.com

The Royal Institute of Chartered Surveyors
Database Resource Centre,
Surveyor Court,
Westwood Way,
Coventry CV4 8JE
Tel: 020 7222 7000   Email: info@ricss.org
Website: www.rics.org

The Royal Institution of Chartered Surveyors in Scotland (RICS Scotland)
9 Manor Place,
Edinburgh EH3 7DN
Tel: 0131 225 7078   Fax: 0131 226 3599
Website: www.rics-scotland.org.uk

The Royal Society of Architects in Wales
Bute Building,
King Edward VII Avenue,
Cathays Park,
Cardiff CF10 3NB
Tel: 029 2087 4753   Fax: 029 2087 4926
Email: wrennm@cf.ac.uk

Royal Society of Ulster Architects
1 Mount Charles,
Belfast, BT7 1NZ
Tel: 01232 323760

The Royal Town Planning Institute
26 Portland Place,
London W1N 4BE
Tel: 020 7636 9107   Fax: 020 7323 1582
Email: online@rtpi.org.uk   Website: www.rtpi.org.uk

Salvo
Tel: 01890 820333. Website: www.salvoweb.com
Organisation of architectural salvage companies.

Save
A conservation charity with a list of homes in need of care and
attention.
www.savebritainsheritage.org

**Scottish and Northern Ireland Plumbing Employers'
Federation**
2 Walker Street,
Edinburgh EH3 7LB
Tel: 0131 2252255

The Scottish Building Employers Federation (SBEF)
Carron Grange,
Carrongrange Avenue,
Stenhousemuir FK5 3BQ
Tel: 01324 555550   Fax: 01324 555551
Email: info@scottishbuilding.co.uk

The Scottish Civic Trust
The Tobacco Merchant's House,
42 Miller Street,
Glasgow G1 1DT
Tel: 0141 221 1466   Fax: 0141 248 6952
Email: sct@scotnet.co.uk   Website: www.scotnet.co.uk/sct

The Society for Protection of Ancient Buildings
37 Spital Square,
London E1 6DY
Tel: 020 7377 1644   Fax: 020 7247 5296
Email: info@spab.org.uk   Website www.spab.org.uk

Solicitors Property Group
c/o Funnel and Perring,
192–193 Queens Road,
Hastings TN34 1RG
Tel: 01424 426287   Fax: 01424 434372

The Stationery Office Publications Centre
PO Box 29,
Norwich NR3 1GN
Tel: 08706 005522   Fax: 08706 005533
Email: book.enquiries@theso.co.uk   Website: www.ukstate.com

The Telecommunications Industry Association
Douglas House,
32–34 Simpson Road,
Fenny Stratford,
Bletchley,
Milton Keynes,
Bucks MK1 1BA
Tel: 01908 645000   Fax: 01908 632263
Email: info@tia.org.uk

Timber and Brick Homes Information Council
Gable House,
40 High Street,
Rickmansworth,
Hertfordshire WD1 3ES
Tel: 01923 778136   Fax: 01923 720724

Twentieth Century Society
Tel: 020 7250 3857

Victorian Society
1 Priory Gardens,
Bedford Park,
London W4 1TT
Tel: 020 8994 1019   Website: www.victorian-society.org.uk

What House? **Magazine**
Blendon Communications Ltd,
207 Providence Square,
Mill Street,
london SE1 2EW
Tel: 020 7939 9888
Website: www.whathouse.co.uk

Useful websites

Property websites

www.08004homes.com
www.asertahome.com
www.asserta.co.uk
www.easier.co.uk
www.estateagent.co.uk
www.findaproperty.com
www.fish4homes.co.uk
www.homes-on-line.com
www.homepages.co.uk
www.hometrack.co.uk
www.move.co.uk
www.properties-direct.com
www.propertyfinder.co.uk
www.propertymarket.co.uk
www.propertyworld.co.uk
www.rightmove.co.uk
www.ukpropertychannel.com
www.upmystreet.com
www.wotproperty.co.uk

Financial websites

www.financelink.co.uk
www.ftyourmoney.com
www.moneyextra.com
www.moneynet.co.uk
www.moneyquest.co.uk
www.thomweb.co.uk
www.yourmortgage.co.uk

Index